STRATEGIC
COMMUNICATION

STRATEGIC
COMMUNICATION

BURTON KAPLAN

THE ART OF MAKING YOUR IDEAS THEIR IDEAS

HarperBusiness
A Division of
HarperCollins*Publishers*

The excerpt on p. 4 from the text of an address by Ed Artzt before the Wharton Graduate School of Business is used with permission.

The speech on p. 200 by Wayne Calloway is used with permission and is held in copyright © 1990 by PepsiCo, Inc.

Library of Congress Cataloging-in-Publication Data

Kaplan, Burton, 1935–
    Strategic communication: the art of making your ideas their ideas/
Burton Kaplan.
      p. cm.
    Includes index.
    1. Business communication. I. Title
    HF5718.K36   1991
    658.4'5—dc20   91–29129
                                                CIP

ISBN 0–88730–413–3

Printed in the United States of America

91 92 93 94 CC/HC 7 6 5 4 3 2 1

For Anna and Leo
L'Chaim

CONTENTS

ACKNOWLEDGMENTS

In his monumental thirty-eighth sonnet, William Shakespeare wrote the definitive author's acknowledgment. Said he,

> If my slight Muse do please these curious days,
> The pain be mine, but thine shall be the praise.

What remains is for me to identify to whom the praise should be directed.

First, to my clients, with and from whom I have learned what you will discover in these pages. Their unfaltering faith throughout the preparation of this book has been both succor and challenge: Michael Lorelli and Craig Weatherup—of Pepsi-Cola Company; Roger Enrico and Lloyd Ward of Frito-Lay; Robert Goehring of Pratt & Whitney; and Ed Artzt and Philip Wieting of Procter & Gamble.

No less in the way of strategic encouragement has come from my agent, John L. Hochmann, whose buoyant spirit proved more compelling than the beckoning border of a dark country, and from my caring editor and patient publisher at HarperCollins, Virginia A. Smith and Mark Greenberg, respectively.

Praise, too, for the comfort of friends—the best of all strategic communicators—without whom my life would seem no more than a footprint in the sea: Dan and Susan Altman, Jeff Ashenberg, Jo Cobb, Angela Freytag, Mary Anne and Edward Gartland, Kirpal Gordon, Susan and Peter Green, The Honorable Elinor Reiner, Richard Reiser, Elinor and Harold Schapiro, and Roger Shelley.

And finally, particular thanks to my family, especially my daughter Lesley, who graces my life with her shining spirit.

IF YOU WANT TO RUN THE SHOW

PART I

1

THE MAGIC PILL

Up has its down, and in its out, but as for communication there is no opposite.

None of us—not you, not me, not anybody—cannot *not* communicate on the job. That's because communication is inevitable. Everything we say or don't say affects others. It either contributes to our business success or hinders it.

An example:

As senior communication consultant to Revlon top management, I wrote the CEO's "calling card," the corporate annual report. Each year, as the deadline drew near, I called on the presidents of the various operating divisions to discuss the project.

The office of the head of the domestic beauty division presented a particular problem. A secretary, let's call her Darlene, was the keeper of the gate. Despite extreme deadline urgency, Darlene was steadfastly uncooperative. Time after time, I was forced to cool my heels in an outer office while she busied herself with projects that were unlikely to be as important or timely. She once had the chutzpa to repair a broken fingernail before acknowledging I was even there. I waited in silence, at least for a while, but my very presence was an unmistakable call for attention. She could not *not* respond, even if only to make me more uncomfortable by further ignoring me.

Up the line, down the line—you name it and Darlene clones are everywhere. They're part of everybody's everyday life in the workplace. Yet some rising managers, people like you in jobs like yours, fail to see them for what they are: experts in the art of getting a message across. That's because they regard as gospel the idea that communication takes place only when it is planned, successful, and positive—an immaculate misconception if ever there was one!

Communication goes on no matter what, whether you connect or not, speak or hold your tongue, intend it or don't, act or remain passive. That makes communication, the process by which your ideas become their ideas, the universal glue. Not only does it bind employee to organization, stockholder to company, and buyer to seller, it bonds managers at every level to their peers, subordinates, and superiors.

"If you want to run the show someday and run it well, you had better learn to think, write, and speak—in that order—clearly, forcefully, concisely, and to the point."

The speaker is Ed Artzt, Procter & Gamble's CEO. He's speaking—a euphemism for recruiting—at the Wharton Graduate School of Business at the University of Pennsylvania:

"You can learn how to do that. At P&G, we teach people to do that. We think it expands a manager's capacity enormously if he communicates well. We also think that an organization has a much better chance of beating the competition if people really understand what they are saying to each other and, occasionally, understand what the boss is saying to the organization. . . .

"I recall one time many years ago when a young man in my brand group, relatively new with Procter & Gamble, wrote a two-page memorandum proposing that our company develop and market our first liquid household cleaner. The proposal was forceful, persuasive, and articulate. It made points clearly and with appropriate understatement. It was approved.

"A day later, Neil McElroy, the chairman of the board, appeared in the darkness of my doorway. I didn't have windows in my office then. He had the memo with him.

" 'Can this young man really think this well?' he asked.

" 'Yes,' I said. 'That's his thinking.'

" 'Well then, why don't we promote him?' Mr. McElroy asked me.

"We did, and he did well, and I received a strong commendation from my boss for my role in training him to communicate his thinking so well.

"I've never forgotten that illustration of the power of good communication in the management process. This young fellow, who had been with the company just a short time, had, with the power of two pages of written communication, convinced the company to take a major initiative in a new business when it already controlled the market. We all felt like winners that day, believe me."

Once upon a time, communication was shorthand for one of three things: find out, point out, or cry out. Needs were urgent, subjects uncomplicated, and everybody was a Dale Carnegie.

It is true that in today's more organized social structure we rely less on communication as a means to survive. It is equally true that in a world grown bewilderingly complex we rely on it even more to prevail. Communication, the key to social transformation, is *the* lever of personal progress.

Now as never before, your career, and those of the rising managers you compete with, cannot possibly reach critical mass without the ability to communicate *successfully* with decision makers. These decision makers, meanwhile, would like nothing more than to be shown how your ideas contribute to the organization's mission.

Despite the obvious mutuality, rising managers say that trying to get through can be an exercise in shouting down the wrong end of the megaphone.

The difficulty lies almost as much with the senior management side of things as with the rising managers themselves. Inevitably, as careers head north, leadership concerns spread east and west. Issues you bring your superiors rarely amount to more than a minor blip on their horizon. Among other things, this ignites competition for a share of the head honcho's time—the only business resource that, once used, can never be replenished. You've seen the consequences: Open time on a corner-office calendar is like fresh blood in the water—a predictable way to draw sharks.

So much for the rock.

Now consider the hard place.

Rising managers don't know how to make effective use of the time senior management does grant!

For the most part, they simply never learned how to win and hold support for their ideas. It is common knowledge that success often turns on the power to persuade, inform, and inspire others.

All the same, myopic colleges and graduate schools blindly stress not the ability to get your ideas across but the ability to get ideas, period. Considering that rising managers aren't taught to communicate, it's no wonder the top echelon sees them as victims of their own educations.

The problems of limited access and educated incapacity add up to an unsettling double whammy. Yet they are far from the only obstacles dogging a rising manager out to make his or her ideas their ideas.

Successful communication means one thought held in common. But minds miss more often than meet. The question is, Why?

What prevents an appreciation for your views and plans among the people—your peers, superiors, subordinates—who stand to benefit the most from them? What locks the sword of understanding in the stone of indifference?

I think the best way to get a handle on the issue is to recognize, first of all, that most people's view of communication is unconsciously conditioned by our sound bite culture.

Thanks in part to the baleful influence of the media, we have become a terribly impatient society. It seems there's never enough time to do things right (but, somehow, always enough time to do them over). To cope, we're too often glib when we shouldn't be. People who watch the evening news see hurricanes chew through entire tropical islands in 60 seconds or less and judge presidential candidates on isolated phrases. We're tuned to uptake information more quickly than our parents and light-years faster than their parents. Slogans and statistics have become more important than the ideas and events they are supposed to represent. "I think Mrs. Reagan thought the 'Just Say No' thing was national and effective," observes former NBC president Grant Tinker. "It wasn't; it was just a lapel button."

Nowhere is it written that catchwords are inherently counterproductive, but over the long run they subliminally condition what gets said and the way in which many of us elect to say it.

All of this wouldn't amount to much if people were perfectly consistent—if they swallowed communication on the job in the same passive, mindless, and accepting way they eat up TV news in their living rooms. There would never be any difficulty getting through. No conflicting attitudes. No distracting emotions. No secret lives. No egos to contend with.

But they don't.

Robots accept business ideas without question. Not so humanity.

With all of their imagination, curiosity, sensitivity, and rich inner life, your coworkers are rarely satisfied by bald statements of fact delivered in twenty-word bursts.

Even all-pervading impatience—a hurry-up state of mind—does not fully explain the unnerving difficulty rising managers encounter in the struggle to win and hold support for their ideas. If that were not the case, if expansiveness was all it took to get through, we'd prattle on for hours, write volumes instead of memos, and you wouldn't be reading this book. But let's be honest. Tomes often prove no better at communicating than telegrams. No, length alone is not the answer. Something else, some complicating factor, is at work here. To understand it, we need to probe the nature of communication itself.

You see, once we allow ourselves to become victimized by a headline mentality, we assume an "as if" view of things.

- We act as if communication is a one-way street running from us to them—with no return flow.
- We operate as if we are the only thing happening to the listener at the moment.
- We function as if what we say and do are the sole determinants of the other guy's reactions.

As a consequence, unskilled communicators become so focused on *what* to say they ignore the even more crucial problem: How to get the other guys to listen in the first place, to put their needs aside for a moment to consider ours.

Here's a for instance. The scene is the corporate cafeteria. A couple of young managers take the table next to mine.

"I finally got that summer intern we've been after," announces the first. He's a finance type I'll call Delaney. "Human Resources called a little while ago. She'll be here the first week in June so I think we ought to use lunch today to make some plans."

"The first Monday? In June?" Delaney's lunch partner, a guy named Castle, does a double take. "How about that! The week of the Pebble Beach conference. Say, do you remember last year when I shot a thirty-eight on the back nine?"

"Her name's Melanie Deansworth and she's number two in her class at Wharton."

" . . . I'll never forget it: You were down to your last ball when you dribbled one off the tee. You sure looked silly racing it to the water . . . and winning! Hold the phone, Delaney. Did you say Wharton? That's in Philly, isn't it?"

"What of it?"

"Well, it's just that right outside of Philly's where that pro shop I told you about is. The one makes golf shoes."

"Castle!" The impatience in Delaney's voice floats my way loud and clear. "Her MBA's in finance. Second in her class, supposed to be a joy to work with."

"So, what size do you wear?"

"Say again?"

"Size. Hey, are you listening or what? Golf shoes, Delaney, golf shoes! What size golf shoes you wear?"

"Golf shoes? I thought we were discussing interns!"

Human communication thrives on the satisfaction of mutual needs—always has and always will. "No man is an island unto himself," wrote the greatest poet of his age, John Donne. Nearly four hundred years later, Donne's words still remind us of the needs we harbor but cannot possibly satisfy alone—for acceptance, for admiration, for reassurance, and for respect. These are satisfied all kinds of ways, most of them involving communication. Even when a conversation is not dedicated to their fulfillment, needs slip through like water from a cupped palm.

Seen in this light, effective on-the-job communication—not just shared words but shared *understanding*—pivots on the ability to identify with the needs of the other guy.

If this begins to suggest that a communication is really a relationship, go to the head of the class!

A communication *is* a relationship.

It bridges the most formidable distance of all, the one between two minds. And as the song says, "It Takes Two to Tango." *Both* sides have to want it equally. There's no making up with unilateral *fortissimo* what's lacking in bilateral *simpatico*.

Communication works when each party satisfies the unfilled needs of the other side. At its best this yields a pooling of information, a shared interest, or a coming together of views. And at its worst, another lost opportunity.

On the remote chance that what you have just read does not compute, let me put the proposition plain:

To communicate is to shape concepts, language, and style in ways that simultaneously satisfy the desires of the communicator and the *unfilled* needs of the audience.

Having recognized what makes a communication a communication, a qualm still obtains.

How do you make it happen?

Where's the leverage to pull the sword from the stone?

In a word, the leverage is *strategy.*

Think about that for a minute, and here's where logic and reason lead:

The problem of relating a communication to the unfilled needs of an audience is no different than the problem of creating a product to suit the unfilled needs of a market.

Or shaping a sales drive to satisfy the requirements of a distribution system.

Or creating an advertising campaign to correspond to consumer demographics.

They're all examples of business strategy at work to establish a proper fit between sellers and buyers.

More than compelling arguments, more than writing ability, more, in fact, than almost anything else, it is the quality of the fit that makes success—in our case, shared thought—possible.

Which is what this book is all about. It formulates a powerful new system of business communication where none existed before—a system driven by the belief that effective communication develops best and most consistently from an orderly structure we call strategy.

Strategy is the framework that obliges you to make choices about what to say and how to say it, in ways that are faithful to your goals and the needs of your audience.

From this emerges the competitive edge your career needs for critical mass—the power to win and hold instant support for your ideas.

Step-by-step, you will learn to tailor a strategy to meet any and every business situation. Each development is amplified by honest-to-business examples you can follow and be guided by.

There are no alphabet-soup formulas to memorize.

No paint-by-the-numbers thinking to get between you and the people you mean to affect.

Instead, you'll find an interactive system of surefire *skills.*

They work *every* time, without fail. And once you learn them, they apply to all your communication needs—on the phone or in person, on paper or on your feet.

What you bring to the party are simple things, most of which you already know. The ability to think things out. The knack of writing things down. The wisdom never to shoot from the lip. What we are talking about, really, is common sense and sound business judgment. The rest will come easily as we move along.

What strategic communication offers in return is this assurance: Never again will you have to struggle to make your ideas heard by shouting them down the wrong end of the megaphone.

Thinking back over decades spent as a typewriter-for-hire, I can recall people coming to me in search of a magic pill—something to instantly confer the ability to communicate.

I always told them no such pill existed.

Well, I was wrong. Dead wrong.

It does exist.

That's right, today there is a pill you can take to make your ideas their ideas.

It just takes several hundred pages to swallow.

2

A STRATEGIC SNAPSHOT

One of the ironies of modern business lies in the difference between being right and being successful.

When you stop to think about it, you, me—in fact, most of us—are right most of the time. If that were not the case, if our business judgment wasn't on target at least two times out of three, we'd be looking for jobs instead of looking to advance our careers. Still, right though we may be, most of us never rise to the very top of our organizations. Somewhere on our drive to a corner office we bump up against a glass ceiling. At that point, what should always have been obvious suddenly becomes clear.

It is better to be right than wrong but that doesn't make being right the sine qua non of personal progress.

In a way, it is a crying shame. If we're going to the trouble of being so all-fired correct in the first place, how come, like Nobel prize-winner Albert Camus, most of us eventually have to confront the disturbing truth about the one and only trouble with our future: It never turns out to be what it once was!

The explanation is summed up in a six-letter word: people. Early in our careers, when we were still relatively wet behind the ears, we were judged mainly on our ability to perform as individuals. That's when being correct in our views and judgments was the heartbeat of progress.

On becoming rising managers not only did the pulse and the pace quicken, people outside of ourselves began to complicate matters. To begin with, we could no longer be everywhere we

11

needed to be in person. That meant we had to find a way to extend our presence and success became less a matter of what we ourselves did than what we were able to oblige others to do on our behalf.

So much for Leadership 101.

The point I make here is one of those truths that's so self-evident it is often overlooked.

As rising managers, we are a growth company outperforming the market in which we compete. So far so good. Now comes the catch. Our "business" can grow only to the extent our sole employee continues to grow in talent, skill, and ability. That's something we cannot experience without the willing and active cooperation of the people we work for and with. Remember, it is only through people that we are invited and, yes, empowered, to reach ever deeper within ourselves to become what we may be capable of. That makes the ability to persuade, inspire, and inform our peers, our superiors, and our subordinates critical. If we expect to get anywhere as rising managers, anywhere at all, we need to act as if our very livelihood depends on the skill with which we make our ideas their ideas.

Certainly, the ideas have to be right in our own minds, but that's not all they have to be. If they are to get through, if they are to actually contribute to the forward momentum of our careers, they have to be just as right in the other guy's mind.

What really counts, in other words, is less a matter of being correct than of being perceived by others to be correct. Because unless and until your peers, subordinates, and superiors believe you to be right, you might as well be wrong. Fail to convince them, and you can't emerge the beneficiary of your own wisdom.

That is why, in strategic terms, it is important to recognize a business communication not as a discrete event but as a continuous process, part of a sequence of discrete events. These are driven less by facts than by the complex interplay—the fit—between communicator and audience. The quality of the fit is what determines the difference between speaking and being heard, between hollow words and shared ideas.

Strategy manages the fit. Like a disciplined master tailor, it drives you to take up a little here and let out a little there—all the time shaping ideas to the mind-set of the audience. Altogether it involves dozens, maybe hundreds, of little acts of communication.

Each small success extends the chain reaction that eventually begets understanding.

Through the careful application of four basic skills of strategy—eliciting other people's thoughts, defusing their emotions, providing them with feedback, overcoming their resistance—we encourage the mutual respect that triggers acceptance of our point of view. Sure, more rides on some components than on others. But what really determines critical mass, the point at which minds touch, isn't one particular concept or the intensity of any one set of words so much as the context within which we place those words and the steady buildup of acceptance the context inspires.

Because, in the end, mutual trust is what eventually bridges that most formidable gap of all, the one between two minds. Strategic thinking zeroes in on the other guys. It filters your insights through the mesh of their wants, needs, and wishes. This establishes a framework to shape concepts, language, and style in ways that simultaneously satisfy your desires *and* the unfilled needs of your audience.

Figure 2.1 shows what I mean.

The whole idea is to key on strategic principles, not tactics. To develop strategies centered on:
• Target audience identity
• Communication objective
• Message
• Tonality

Each of these elements raises a specific question about one or another aspect of your communication.
• With whom am I talking?
• What do I want from them?
• How will I get it?
• What is the overall impression I wish to create?

Your answers are the invisible hand that guides and shapes everything about your communication, written or spoken, planned or impromptu. They reveal whether you are talking with everybody in general or someone specific; seeking to clarify an issue, sell a new concept, argue for a bigger budget, or resolve a dispute; appealing to reason purely on a rational basis or injecting an element of emotion.

The invisible hand—that's longhand for strategy—is the

STRATEGIC PROCESS

Communicator Wants	Communication Strategy	Audience Wants
Profile	Target Audience Definition	Recognition
Solution	Communications Objective	Unfilled Needs Satisfied
Leverage	Message	Rationale for Action
Environment for Success	Tonality	Unequivocal Clarity

Figure 2.1. The objective of the strategic process is to establish a proper fit between communicator and audience. A communication strategy provides an orderly framework to shape concepts, language, and style in ways that simultaneously satisfy the desires of the communicator and the unfilled needs of the audience.

framework, the game plan. You use it to solve a specific problem in communication, written or spoken, no matter who is on the other end of the line.

And there you have it—a snapshot of strategic communication.

The rest of this book is going to develop the image, strategy by strategy.

3

THE TARGET AUDIENCE

90 PERCENT LOGIC AND
THE OTHER HALF IS EMOTION

A rising manager's most valuable skill has less to do with the ability to create work product than with the ability to create understanding.

"The complex undertakings of modern life depend on the cooperation of many people with different specialties in different places," argues culture maven E. D. Hirsch. "Where communications fail, so do the undertakings."

Accordingly, Hirsch reasons, leaders develop their ambitions best by developing the ability to communicate—to persuade, inform, and inspire others.

By recognizing the premium on communication skills Hirsch illuminates a proposition that's as old as the Bible. Ever since the Tower of Babel we've known that when a communication does not relate to the audience, the audience can't relate to the communication.

That being the case, only one question remains: What makes a communication appropriate to its audience? In other words, What really drives successful communication?

Untutored opinion is mixed. Some think the horsepower is a matter of lofty language. Others will tell you a certain clarity of mind kicks up the octane rating.

Both positions are about as right as they are wrong.

The ability to communicate has less to do with creating noble language than with creating language that the people you want to reach *can accept as their own.* Think about the implications of that

15

last sentence, about the fact that the way to really talk to others is to talk like others, and what reveals itself is a notion strong enough to jump-start a career:

Whether they are customers or colleagues, everybody on the receiving end wants to feel that what you have to say relates to what is already on their minds.

Discerning what is already on their minds is, of course, the linchpin of communication success. As we explore in the pages immediately ahead the strategic means to analyze the other guy's identity, bear in mind that the reason your ideas become their ideas has nothing to do with your setting them an example. Not at all. It happens because you make it appear as though you follow their example. There is only one bit of intelligence that enables you to do that and it is tack-sharp knowledge of the other side's innermost workings: what they feel and what they believe.

The man who demonstrated to me for the first time the power that comes of knowing your target audience—knowing them in some ways better even than they know themselves—was the founder of the Revlon cosmetics empire, the late Charles Revson.

Charles drove home the idea that, no matter what the message, no matter what the medium, people everywhere communicate and need to be communicated with on two levels simultaneously. One of those levels is logic and the other is emotion. Hoping to get through by satisfying one or the other, Charles maintained, is certain to produce results as predictable as anything in Pavlov.

With the unrivaled power to communicate, the former fabric salesman from rural New Hampshire showed a waiting world how reaching people—making his ideas their ideas—could turn a hank of hair and a hunk of color into bankable gold.

I once asked him to tell me what made Revlon communications so compelling. Surely it was not the pictures—every cosmetics ad had an elegant picture. Nor could it be the words; everybody's copy silently implied what Philip Wylie, author of "A Generation of Vipers," proclaimed to be the real message of all cosmetic advertising: This product promises to make you a better lay.

So what was the secret of communication that grabbed women and never let them go?

I had no sooner spoken the question than Charles turned his relentless glare my way. His eyelids narrowed but only for an instant. Abruptly, he rose from the chair in which he was seated and left the room without speaking another word. With Revson, life was a zero-sum game: You were either his main man or an obstruction. It didn't look as though I was anybody's main man. And everybody knew what Charles did about obstructions.

Several worrisome days later I was summoned to his office and as I approached it, figured the end was at hand.

Occupying the entire northwest corner of the General Motors Building's 49th floor, his lavish suite comprised several thousand square feet and overlooked most of New York's Central Park. Here, in an Empire ambiance of dark woods, noble brasses, pale carpets, and lustrous silks, Mr. Charles held court.

As I cooled my heels at the open doorway to the richly appointed inner sanctum, I overheard the tail end of a verbal flogging. Taking the lash was a fellow I'll call Harrison. Harrison's behavior had always given me the impression the only thing he found worse than being exploited was not being exploited. Hearing the venom in Charles's voice, I cringed at the thought that my turn was next. It was a Harrison with a smile on his face but none in his heart who emerged several minutes later.

Charles motioned for me to draw near his desk.

"Kiddo," he barked, as though days had not intervened between the time I raised the question and now, "don't ever forget that communication is what makes Revlon Revlon. We know how to move a market our way because we know that women are 90 percent logic and the other half is emotion.

"The part that shows is the logical side, the outer self who comes up with answers to questions like, How do I make my job better?

"But behind the issues you can see is the hidden agenda, the emotional side of things that's always asking the question behind the question, How do I get people to love me?

"Nobody's immune to the mix of head and heart. One ties to the other like warp to weft. Subtract either and you drop a stitch. Knit them and bingo!—by plucking heartstrings you get them to open their purse strings!"

It is one thing to learn that the minds you wish to touch both send and receive on two frequencies simultaneously. And quite another to transform that knowledge into a new understanding between you—yours!

Here's where the strategic approach to business communication begins to tilt things your way. It provides the means to examine humanity's context with a watchmaker's eye, learn what makes the other guys tick, and position your thoughts accordingly.

Experience has probably shown you time and again that there is no easy answer to the question, How do I communicate with others?

Over several decades of manager watching, I've seen people like you persuade, inform, and inspire. And about as many times or more, seen otherwise capable managers fall flat on their keisters in the process. It seems to me that the difference between the successes and the also-rans is this:

The ones whose messages get through consistently know something the other folks haven't bothered to learn. What they know is that *ideas can't be pounded in from the outside.*

To grasp an idea in a way that makes it feel safe—the way, for instance, they grasp one of their own—audiences need to feel they can reach for it from within themselves. That being the case, the best messages are like the best sales spiels. Never out to sell anything. Really what they do is just the opposite. They work to create the ultimate leverage—a climate in which prospects sell themselves.

All this is so because communication is something that comes from *within* each person. It isn't anything you can supply directly. In this respect, communication is like growing. You can't *make* children grow but you can supply the nourishment they need to mature physically and emotionally.

Similarly, you can't *make* people communicate, but you can create the kind of climate in which they want to share your thoughts, plans, and ideas. Creating such a climate effectively multiplies the attractiveness of your ideas among the very people you most want to reach because it enables you not merely to track their mind-set but to accurately anticipate their views; not just to present issues but to strategically *position* ideas for success within the context they themselves prefer.

As we explore the emotional and factual sides of the audience in an effort to identify them, it is well to bear in mind that psychologists are not in complete agreement as to how communication occurs. Several variables influence an individual's acceptance of your thoughts. In line with the general belief that people have reasons for doing what they do, it is widely believed that communication arises out of human need. The most important, first of all, being his or her own needs and, second, your behavior in relation to those needs—your understanding of them.

To validate the observation that needs and communication are hand-and-glove, psychological thinkers have directed significant attention to understanding the types of needs that motivate the exchange of thought.

One of the most useful descriptions of human needs as they affect communication was developed by noted social scientist William C. Schutz. His "Theory of Interpersonal Needs" forms the basis for what I call the "Index of Emotional Receptivity"— which I'll explain fully in a moment or two.

Schutz argues that three basic categories of interpersonal needs underlie most human interactions. He identifies these as the *need for inclusion, the need for control,* and *the need for affection.*

According to Schutz, the need for *inclusion* is the need of an individual or group to be singled out, to be noticed, to be recognized as a person or entity distinct from, yet related to, a community of others. Someone with a high need for inclusion might be, say, a bank teller who dresses provocatively in order to draw the spotlight. Meanwhile, people with lower inclusion needs, the wallflowers, prefer to remain in shadow.

Schutz argues that the driving force behind both extremes is the fear of not being recognized: limelighters compensate by actively seeking attention; sideliners convince themselves they will not get attention, and say that is what they prefer.

Chrysler CEO Lee Iacocca and computer whizbang Steve Jobs, for example, combat their inner fear of unimportance by forcing others to pay attention to them. On a scale of 100, Iacocca, Jobs, and people whose work involves sales, product design, advertising, marketing, and show business usually score very high in this dimension.

Meanwhile, at the bottom end of the inclusion index are the people who believe their inner desires for prestige, status, dominance, recognition, attention, importance, and appreciation will never be realized, among them market researchers, plant security executives, and the comptroller's staff.

The need for *control*—the energy driving the sharks with whom you swim daily—reflects a desire to run the show and a hunger to influence the agenda. Ralph Nader, corporate spokespersons, and purchasing agents are part of the cadre deserving a solid 100 here.

Some people enjoy being in charge even if no one is aware

of the role they play. Investment bankers and corporate lawyers, for instance, represent power-behind-the-throne types who are living proof that the need for control and the need for inclusion are not always linked.

The need for control, incidentally, changes as situations and human association evolve. Donald Kendall, for instance, sought recognition from the public at large for his role as businessperson. It was only as an *éminence grise* in the field of commerce that he hid his lamp beneath President Richard Nixon's bushel basket.

Turning now to the need for *affection,* this index reflects the desire to be part of a team. It suggests how close people want to be to others and how much they want and need to be liked.

Human resources managers, telemarketers, men and women concerned with distribution and delivery, and customer service people all score high on this scale. Lower scores are associated with the more independent pursuits of researchers, technical writers, and actuaries, people who prefer the insulation of interpersonal distance.

So, what does it all mean?

Well, for openers, it should be said that Schutz was neither a communication consultant nor a businessperson. He was a social scientist who developed his understanding of the relationship between needs and communication through clinical studies, none of which, to my knowledge, were conducted in a workplace setting.

Nevertheless, it has long been my experience, and that of others, that Schutz's work could help rising managers better understand and communicate with peers, subordinates, and superiors. And, further, *that a view of communication as a process of satisfying unfilled needs* may help managers like you in jobs like yours to create better and more mutually productive communication.

All of which brings us to the Index of Emotional Receptivity I mentioned a few paragraphs back. This index is an informal way to establish a profile of the emotional needs of the people with whom you are in contact. At the same time, this psychological radar plot actually charts the strategic route to make your ideas their ideas.

Here's how it works.

You rate the audience on a scale of 1 to 100 on each of three dimensions of need: the need for inclusion, the need for control, and the need for affection.

In general, the highest scoring variable represents the audience's point of maximum emotional vulnerability. By tailoring your argument to exploit this soft spot you position your views in an emotional context they can relate to and accept.

A score of 100–100–100 offers the widest possible latitude; 1–1–1 makes the task of communicating considerably more difficult.

Three examples illustrate the way the Index of Emotional Receptivity works in practice.

The first concerns Roger Shelton, who manages investor relations for one of the country's larger health-care companies. When the subject is the pharmaceutical industry, Roger is the one the *Wall Street Journal* calls. You may not always agree with his point of view but you never forget who said it. On the need for inclusion Roger scores 90, on the need for control 60, and 30 on the need for affection. This pattern suggests that courting Roger with lavish flattery and shoulder-squeezing bonhomie may seem in order, but the tactic will probably alarm him. Instead, the unspoken message should suggest that the proposition under discussion will make him shine not just in your eyes but in the eyes of his boss.

It is hard to top an up-and-coming manager whose national sport is dotting the eyes and crossing the tees. That's what makes Bob Goehring, head of advertising for Pratt & Whitney's engine division, so fundamentally tough to beat. He scores 30–90–60 on emotional receptivity. With him, the key is not to stress how your idea maximizes the opportunity for success but, rather, how it minimizes the risk of failure.

Among Gillette's cadre of young achievers, Jane Castle is a standout. Fresh out of Dartmouth's Amos Tuck School of Business, Jane is keen on participatory management and team play. I score her 60–30–90 and, accordingly, position my ideas as rallying points for her troops.

What the Index of Emotional Receptivity is to emotions the Range of Factual Possibility is to logic. This predictive yardstick reckons, in advance, the likelihood of an argument to win audience acceptance.

President John F. Kennedy defined politics as the art of the possible. He might well have been talking about communication for here, too, you cannot sell what the market will not buy.

The question is, What's possible?

4

OBJECTIVES AND MESSAGES

THE TWO AND ONLY

When it comes to making your ideas their ideas, your worst enemy probably isn't your worst enemy after all.

Chances are, you are up against an even more formidable adversary—yourself.

Most of us make the mistake of thinking everyone else thinks the way we do. As if that were not sufficiently troublesome, we then compound the problem. We expect others to understand fully what it is we hope and expect to achieve through communication. Never mind that we ourselves do not always fully understand our own intentions.

Attempting to articulate our views before we establish clear objectives is about as safe as skydiving. So long as luck runs our way, everything is hunky-dory. But as failed communicators and the survivors of some parachutists learn, the law of averages eventually exacts a toll.

Your daily life is a world of business communication. You
- Clear a decision with your boss.
- Take a meeting on market share results.
- Telephone a client to set delivery dates.
- Draft a memo on head count.
- Present a new product idea.
- Evaluate the strengths and weaknesses of a competitor's line.
- Redeploy staff.
- Inform a peer.

Each activity involves on-the-job communication. Each communication has a purpose.

The question is, what are the *strategic* purposes of these and the rest of your work-related communication contacts?
- To change a mind-set?
- To affect a decision?
- To motivate subordinates?
- To announce a development?
- To enlist aid or attention?

If you said any of the above you wouldn't be exactly wrong. But neither would you have been truly responsive to the question.

You see, all of these are *tactical* objectives. Meanwhile, the subject of present and watchful concern is *strategic* goals.

So, what's the difference?

Think of it this way:

Strategy is to tactics what game plan is to individual play— the larger concept that gives maneuver its mission. Seen in this light, for instance, the question, What can we do to reduce our head count? is a tactical outgrowth of the more strategic question, What can we do to cut costs?

There's always been a potentially bewildering and often contradictory range of views on the topic of communication objectives. Generalizing now, the most familiar school of thought suggests the largest purpose of every business communication is to sell something—an idea, a point of view, or the personality behind the words. Others, meanwhile, argue that we communicate to test the limits of authority.

I think it's notions like these that lead some people to conclude that business communication, like sports writing, is a contradiction in terms.

Now don't get me wrong. These and other communication rationales may be intellectually acceptable. But more to the point, they are at a remove from the real-world concerns of rising managers. Viewed through the lens of daily business reality they bear not at all on the ultimate strategic priority—managing the fit between the communicator and the communicatee.

Years of working with rising managers like you on the tough business communication issues convinced me that a more useful strategic objective probably existed. I didn't need to invent it. All I had to do was recognize it. And because that is what I set out to discover, that is what experience eventually revealed.

But not without a surprise.

You see, what I sought was a one-size-fits-all theory. It had to meet the measure of every on-the-job communication from casual contact to meaningful meeting.

Though I was blindly groping for a notion I could not crystallize, I knew that in the end my work was going to be worth the effort. Whatever that universal strategic objective turned out to be, it was sure to affect a cascade of decisions.

- The nature of the strategic message
- The tonality of the argument
- The points to be included
- The supporting evidence to be mustered
- And more

Here's where the surprise came in. What I found, what years of practical experience finally made manifest, was this.

There is no one strategic template.

There are two.

That's right.

Thousands of hands-on hours observing some of America's largest and most successful corporations at work convinced me. Every successful business communication that ever was or ever will be serves one of two possible strategic ends.

The discovery was consistent with my overall view of strategic thinking. Strategy, after all, is the management process that determines the direction your communication will take, what it will achieve, and how you get from the here-and-now to the there-and-then. By its very definition, strategy is shorthand for informed selection. You make choices from options. So, rather than feeling disappointed at my failure to discover one unequivocal principle, I felt further confirmed in my belief when I found two.

I had been asked to review a reel of television commercials. The idea was to select the ones I most loved to hate. Two in particular touched an unsympathetic nerve.

The first informed viewers that the long-awaited millennium had arrived. Never again need we suffer the anguish of ring around the collar.

The second developed the way to end the heartbreak of psoriasis.

The laundry commercial brought me news of a new product. On first viewing it made me *aware* of something I had never before known.

On the other hand, the shampoo advertising wasn't out so

much to sell me on a new idea as to *convince* me of the value of an old one.

And there they were—the concepts I had been looking for. The ones that define the objective of every strategic business communication that ever was or will be.

Awareness and *conviction.*

You report to the boss. Isn't that to make her aware of your progress?

You meet with employees to discuss performance reviews. Aren't you out to convince them you've been fair in your evaluation?

Awareness and conviction.

Don't kid yourself. What we're dealing with here is nothing less than strategic bedrock. I've examined thousands of business documents. Analyzed work-related conversations involving hundreds of people like you doing jobs like yours. And what I keep coming away with is a basic tenet of strategic thinking:

What is not intended to create awareness must be intended to create conviction.

Though at first glance the choice between awareness and conviction as your objective may seem less than critical, don't be misled. Strategic outcomes turn on the consistency between your objective and the thought you wish to implant. When your objective is to create awareness but your message deals with conviction, you can practically hear the nail screech across the blackboard. On the other hand, render the subject and object in harmony and what you make can be music to the audience's ears.

I raise this warning because would-be communicators often allow themselves to fall into the trap of treating awareness and conviction as interchangeable parts. Instead of producing a clear and single-minded communication, a message out of sync with its objective is a double signal. And like all equivocation, it confuses more than it compels.

Here's what I mean.

Suppose you are the point person on your purchasing department's vendor relations program. You are out to win the commitment of your suppliers to a more comprehensive just-in-time parts program. Said another way, you are out, really, to create conviction.

Your objective is to convince qualified vendors to adopt a zero-defect mentality.

Given these circumstances, the last thing you want is a message that treats the initiative too matter-of-factly, too much like just another ho-hum news announcement.

On the other hand, let's say you need to get word to your people on the very latest development in your organization's maternity-leave policy. Your goal is to create awareness of the policy update within the target audience. In this case, anything but a crisp just-the-facts presentation is likely to work against mindfulness.

Messages designed to create awareness are essentially one-dimensional propositions. Under this classification, you are likely to be dealing with communications seeking not action but illumination:

- Business reports
- Training materials
- Presentations of new developments or products
- Explanations of specific activities or events

Because the content of messages intended to create awareness is either new or new to the audience at hand, there is probably no built-in audience resistance, no structural disbelief, to contend with. Under these conditions, information is conveyed directly through straightforward presentation, description, or teaching.

Since the idea is to leave the audience with more information, understanding, or skill than it had before your communication, clarity and simplicity mark the message designed to produce awareness.

For example, let's say your senior vice president announced a new incentive policy at a division manager's workshop last week. As a follow-up, each of the division heads, you among them, is expected to explain the impact of the new program to their direct reports.

Would you describe the new incentive policy in terms of

1. Senior management's vision of an empowered body of employees?
2. The potential impact of the new program on the balance sheet?
3. None of the above.

If you chose 3, none of the above, you've probably got the makings of a strategic communicator. That's because you recognize that to be consistent with an objective of awareness, your

message should be crafted to stress the nuts-and-bolts aspects of the program:
- What your managers must do.
- How much time they need to spend.
- And how much help they can expect from, say, Human Resources.

Turning now to messages that seek to *convince,* a different standard applies. Here, the big idea is to position *your* thoughts vis-à-vis *their* mind-set. You want them to embrace your idea in a way that produces specific action. Open their checkbooks, close ranks, take a decision, give recognition—the list is probably endless.

And so are the potential problems.

Messages intended to produce conviction bear an extra burden. Sure, they have to encourage respondents to start doing or thinking one thing. But at the same time, they have to encourage those same respondents to stop doing or thinking another—the very thing that prevents them from agreeing with you in the first place.

Net, net, a message aimed at conviction does double duty: as it works to instill belief on one hand it works to suspend disbelief on the other.

Accordingly, persuasive messages comprise two parts. The first is a convincing argument setting forth what the target should believe or do. The second provides credible support for that argument.

Here's an example.

Your organization decides to relocate its headquarters to New Jersey. You call a press conference. You tell the media, "New York says it is a good place to do business. Well, it isn't."

Few in the audience are likely to be persuaded your organization did the right thing. After all, the reporters know that New York is the belly button of the business world—a lively, vibrant metropolis thousands of companies call home.

But suppose you don't stop with an opening statement. Suppose you go on to support the argument with statistics about failing services, rising taxes, and labor force illiteracy.

That support, those statistics, are what gives the audience the permission it needs to accept and believe the opening statement.

Here is another case in point.

Your team didn't make the numbers this period.

Do you tell the boss you fell short by 3 percent due to factors beyond your control and let it go at that?

Hardly.

What you do is provide her with the support it takes to suspend her disbelief. So you tell her that the soft spot in operating profit before taxes is due entirely to an unbudgeted factory variance caused by higher energy costs.

What you don't know about strategic communication objectives and their effect on messages won't hurt you.

No, not at all.

It will kill you. Or at any rate, kill any chance you might otherwise have to make your idea their idea.

Now I am not saying that the ability to recognize the distinction between the two and only strategic objectives—awareness and conviction—guarantees your message will work.

What it does guarantee, though, is an edge, more of a fighting chance to persuade, inform, and inspire your peers, subordinates, and superiors.

When you turn the page, you'll see what I mean.

5

TONALITY

NO FORKED TONGUES

In the same way it takes more than a good product to make a market, it takes something beyond the right words to make your ideas their ideas.

Sure, the vocabulary you put into play develops your thoughts. But as you may have noticed, meaning doesn't reside so much in words as it does in the context in which those words are placed. Without a proper setting there's no way they can get across an air of authenticity, a spirit of immediacy, or a sense of unspoken consequence.

This raises a major issue: Having made the effort to think through the identity of the target audience and develop a strategic communication objective and message, how can we be sure the words we choose are understood in the way we mean them to be?

The answer is, we can't always be sure.

According to several reliable investigators, only about 500 words are commonly used in everyday nontechnical business communication. Here's the startling part: All in all, these 500 words have some 14,000 definitions, an average of nearly 30 different ways each word is used. Take the word "run."

You run a business.

Run out a string of data.

Calculate run rates.

Run up costs.

Run an idea past your boss.

Run out of time—the list goes on and on.

Because language is an inexact means of sharing ideas, audiences rely on an unstated *system* of nuances, a constellation that goes beyond vocabulary to also include such nonverbal considerations as gesture, timing, communication site, and more, for clues to interpret what you are saying. *Together these constitute a tonality, a mood, that alerts the audience to understand your message in a way that is beyond words.*

Consider one small example of tonality from the experience of President George Bush. As he campaigned for his first term, Bush, a Brahmin, sought to capitalize on the relatively brief period he had spent early in his career in the Lone Star state. Unlikely as it seemed, the idea was for the Texas electorate to accept the New Englander as another good ole boy out of the oil patch.

Midway through the campaign a TV reporter asked how things were going in the Texas effort. In a remark shaped to set a mood Texans could respond to, the ex-Yalie said, "I guess we kicked some ass down there today."

Northern commentators gave his remark the raspberry. On the other hand, the target audience—a breed known to communicate in a patois all its own (for instance, people in Dallas often refer to friends' families as "yermomenemenall")—gave him the votes he needed and sought.

As a rising manager, leveraging tonality is something you do on a daily basis, but probably on an unconscious level. For instance, as a district manager you're asked to explain to your clients a minor change in billing practice. By sending an overnight letter to deliver the news, you'd run the danger of attaching too much urgency to it, creating an atmosphere that raises more questions than answers. Instead, you matter-of-factly integrate the news into your next regular contact. The low-key tone helps your customers put the new policy into proper perspective.

In other words, what you say and the manner in which you present it *fit each other and the audience* as if they were all made for each other.

Imagine that one of your product managers, a very sensitive and creative person, keeps missing deadlines. So you call her to your office. She sits in the visitor's chair while you take a seat behind your desk. As you speak you refer to a document before you. She cannot see what it says. "You've got to get a better handle on things. Your projects are consistently late."

You haven't said anything that isn't true. You've been careful not to attack her personally. After all, you like her. Value the ideas she brings to the business. Want her to perform better. Still, you've created an ominous context for your remarks, one guaranteed to produce defensiveness on her part.

"It sounds like you don't think I am right for the job," she responds.

Now let's try it again. Only this time, let's see what happens when you more actively manage the atmosphere surrounding your remarks.

First of all, since most people consider nonverbal cues more reliable barometers of intent than words, you go to her office; take the visitor's chair; leave your papers behind on your desk; and, finally, accept her offer of a cup of coffee.

"Basically, Jill, you've done a great job on new product development," you begin. "Still, I am a little concerned about all those missed deadlines. I know you are serious about your work. What can I do to help avoid the slippage?"

She responds. "Well, I'm having trouble with the priorities the lab assigns to my projects. With your clout, what do you say the two of us go over there to see if we can't break the logjam once and for all?"

This honest-to-business example illustrates the difference *managing* the tonality makes.

By entering her personal space you give up the territorial advantage that suggests you hold power over her. True, you might feel more at ease on your home turf but you know that in this case, the name of the game is to reduce her tensions.

Further raising her comfort index are, first, the absence of a list of transgressions and second, the nonverbal signal you send by agreeing to a cup of coffee. A shared pleasure, commonplace though it may be, humanizes the moment and helps defuse the boss–subordinate confrontation.

And finally, by sandwiching a slab of criticism between a couple of slices of praise you effectively communicate two things. Your concern. And your belief in her ability to perform professionally to your standards.

As the experience with Jill suggests, there are no simple solutions to the challenges of tonality. No one-dimensional Psychology 101 prescriptions to intensify the power of your ideas.

The key is to see each situation on its own merits. To bring to each the interactive mix of individual elements it needs and deserves.

Like other aspects of strategic communication, an effective tonality derives from a combination of several elements: your knowledge of the target audience; the objective you seek to attain; the site in which the communication takes place; and the means, written or oral, by which you make your thoughts known.

In the present chapter we'll limit our examination to the universal factors. The ones that apply whether you are communicating on the phone or in person, on paper or on your feet. Later, as appropriate, we'll take up such specifics as the effect of timing, space, body language, and silence on tonality.

Meanwhile, the first consideration in striking the right tonality is to determine the overall impression you seek to make upon the audience. Do you wish to sound forceful or passive, personal or impersonal, colorful or colorless, crisp or engaging?

Your answers to these and like questions should, first of all, reflect the nature of your relationship to the audience. Are you colleagues or strangers, peers or unequal?

Think of it this way: If a coworker who is also a friend asks you to read and evaluate a document he prepared, he would find it inappropriate if it came back with a note beginning, "Your report is returned herewith."

On the other hand, communications directed to top management should be somewhat more formal than, "Phyllis, when I saw you at the bar last night . . ." Among old friends, you can safely choose to express your ideas in ways that are warmer, friendlier, and more engaging than if you are in contact with the top brass of a very large and status-conscious organization.

The next step is to put yourself into the audience's shoes. If you were they, if you saw the subject through their eyes, what would you expect and how would you prefer to receive it? Your answers help you develop the empathy it takes to avoid a self-centered presentation. They constrain you to select language and examples that are consistent with the wishes, hopes, and preferences of the people you seek to persuade, inspire, or inform.

When the objective of your communication is to create awareness, the tonality of your communication should seek to establish a rational, more or less matter-of-fact air.

Accordingly, you support this rational model best through an air of dispassionate credibility. The combination of understatement and balance helps create the impression that you have carefully examined the issues to arrive at an intelligent, informed, and largely neutral point of view.

To add to the steady buildup of credibility, the language you employ to articulate your thoughts is crisp, definite, concrete, and specific.

Compared with communications intended to produce awareness, those aimed at convincing others to do or think or act in a certain way are 180 degrees out. They require a more personal and emotional tonal approach.

Bear with me for a minute while I explain.

In a factual presentation the accent falls more on messages than on messengers.

The opposite is true when you are out to promote conviction. Here, the presenter leaves the background to become every bit as important as the ideas being presented.

Generally speaking, then, the key to a convincing tonality is a measure of emotional openness. How open? Sufficient to establish the authenticity of the communicator.

This premise—to share how you feel about what you are saying or writing—rests on the notion that none of us is unique. What we see, others can see. What we feel, others have felt. Thoughts, phrases, and gestures that affect your level of conviction can, and often do, touch sympathetic nerves in others.

"Have you ever gotten the feeling that your world is shrinking to the narrow confines of your job description?" These opening words set the tonality of my friend Kevin Dedrick's recent letter of resignation. "I have, and I want to tell you about it."

Dedrick really liked his job and his boss. For several years, though, he felt boxed in. When a vice presidential spot opened at a vendor company, he could no longer resist. As a matter of enlightened self-interest, he wished to convince his old boss how much he cared for the organization.

"It is hard for me to say goodbye because part of me is not really going anyplace. I may be moving on but I am leaving a large part of my success with you through the people all over this company who made my progress here possible. Through them, part of me will always be part of you."

By creating an atmosphere in which he plainly made his success their success, Kevin showed a deep and abiding feeling for his old company. It came across a hundred percent sincere.

In the largest sense, the whole idea of strategic tonality, it seems to me, honors the first commandment of management:

Thou shalt not create surprises.

When you stop to think about it, that's what professional management is really all about: Establishing a predictable surprise-free climate.

As rising managers, we are conditioned not only to anticipate problems but to correct them before they sneak into our work. Later, senior management measures us by our ability to actually deliver on our plans, surprise-free.

Seen in this context, a business message in conflict with its mood is more than an equivocation. It is, in fact, nothing less than a surprise.

The inconsistency catches its audience off-guard.

Ambiguity stops them cold! Sets off silent alarms.

And the lack of coherence? It makes them wonder what to believe: The content of your message? Or the conflicting context in which you place it?

And with that—pfffft!—there goes receptivity, right down the tube!

Striking the right tonality doesn't just happen. You have to work at it. But in the end, it makes the difference between words that merely read right and a communication that really rings true.

Tonality.

It's the part of strategy that makes sure what you preach is what you practice.

ONE ON ONE

PART II

6

WHAT WORKS AGAINST A MEETING OF THE MINDS

A BASSACKWARD STATE OF AFFAIRS

Organizational scholar and consultant Warren Bennis recounts a favorite baseball story, the tale of the umpire.

> It is the ninth inning of a key playoff game. The count is three-and-two on the batter. The pitcher winds up, kicks. At 96 miles-an-hour his fastball slams into the catcher's mitt.
> The umpire hesitates for a split second in making the call.
> The tense batter whirls around and says, "Well, what the hell was it?"
> "It ain't nothin'," the umpire snarls back, "till I call it!"

To make their dreams apparent to others and to align people with them, leaders—those who are and those who would be—need to be able to communicate their vision.

No matter how self-apparent it may seem, no vision explains itself. The manager-as-leader must be able to make the vision manifest to others. Not merely explain it or clarify it but, like Bennis's umpire, create its meaning.

Accordingly, the truest responsibility of leadership is to make their ideas our ideas.

It is not something that comes easily to any of us.

Expert opinion holds that roughly 80 percent of the people who fail to achieve career goals do so for but one reason: They are unable to create meaning that others can share. If this were not the case, if communication were a natural and not a learned response, how come we study the subject so tenaciously?

39

Write so many books about it?

More to the point, buy and read so many books about it?

We do it because we know that if we are to experience the metamorphosis that turns managers into leaders, it is essential to bridge the gap that separates us from one another and what is from what might be.

It is a self-evident truth that managers flourish with open, clear, sensitive communication. And founder when communication is guarded, hostile, and otherwise ineffective. Given that, and the irrefutable fact that the urge to communicate is not just part of the human condition, it *is* the human condition, how come, wittingly or un-, we make things so difficult?

What's worse, how come we make it even more difficult than we realize?

What prevents us from simply saying what we mean in order to get what we want?

Several barriers stand in the way of conversational communication. Those we create ourselves. And those created by others.

To explain the self-imposed impediment first, we turn to nineteenth-century economist Thorstein Veblen. He coined the phrase, educated incapacity. This is the inability to understand real-life issues we could more easily recognize had we not received our advanced educations. As youngsters, my daughters Tracey and Lesley, for instance, were trained in math class to think in other than base-10 terms but had trouble making change for a dollar.

In the present instance, we are talking about an educated incapacity of mythic proportions—the myth that says, If we can talk we can communicate.

It is an idea that people need or want to be true because it would be bewildering if they were to admit it is not. False though it may be, it has come to be accepted as the conventional wisdom by educated, hands-on managers who should know better. The myth misleads us into thinking that getting through is, if not easy, then certainly less difficult than people like me make it out to be.

I maintain that most rising managers take the ability to communicate for granted. Because they do not bother to understand adequately the ins and outs of the process, they are blind to the problems they themselves create and face in the effort to share thoughts, ideas, and plans. Accordingly, their view is often topsy-turvy. Among other things, they mistake a lack of opposition for agreement (which is bad enough). And the presence of resistance to mean rejection (which is worse).

Let me explain.

Psychologists tell us that in order to be persuaded to another's way of thinking it is both natural and necessary to pass first through a stage of resistance. The resistance arises from our having to give up the position we already hold. If our minds were empty to begin with, we'd accept in a trice every new idea to come down the pike. They would rush in to fill the vacuum.

But adult minds are never empty. What was it my father used to say? "Two adults? Three opinions!"

Pop was right. Not only have we grown-ups got opinions on everything, we've got opinions on opinions.

Let's say you need to persuade one of your direct reports to take a course in statistics. The person may nod, agree that it is a good idea, and then do nothing. Something inside opposes the idea of going back to school. He may feel uncomfortable about returning to the classroom. Or reluctant to give up the time.

Still, he doesn't argue, doesn't engage you in dialogue. If he did, he'd have to give up his proscription and accept your prescription. That frightens him. Silence, therefore, insulates him from what he fears most—the uncertainty of change.

The absence of unbridled resistance only appears to be agreement. What it really amounts to is the sullen silence of lip service. By giving an outward indication of compliance, he cuts off discussion.

Net, net, what appears to be acceptance is really rejection.

But suppose that instead of silence or self-serving sanctimony he actively opposes you with a counterargument. Wham! Bam! Whatever line of reasoning he takes—good, bad, or indifferent—it tells you something within him is responding to your proposition. Partly he feels what you say makes sense. Meanwhile, the part of him that abhors school fights you tooth and nail. His struggle to convince you is a sure sign he is fully involved in your thought and not entirely comfortable with his own.

In other words, his very resistance signals not the rejection of your communication but its penetration.

Given the apparently bassackward state of affairs wherein a yes can be a no, and a no might really mean maybe, the wonder is not that business communication is difficult but that it goes on as well as it does!

So much for the self-imposed behaviors we place in the way of communication. I'd like to draw your attention next to the impediments imposed by others. I am referring to the roadblocks rising managers like you encounter, one-on-one, on the phone, in a conference, in conversation over lunch, in casual meetings in the hallway, in giving and getting direction, in annual performance reviews, job interviews, negotiations.

If our audiences were machines we'd never have any difficulty getting through. We'd have no conflicting attitudes, emotional distractions, secrets, or ego to contend with. These ever-present human tendencies work against communication. Operating below the level of awareness, they turn on tension and force focus inward, away from us, from our words, from the very things we seek to get across.

Barriers come in all kinds of incarnations. For the sake of your time, I've boiled these down to five communication spoilers.

First is *resistance to change.*

We are all caught in a web of habit. The web feels safe because we are both the spider and the fly. We cling to established ways of thinking, feeling, and acting for several good reasons. Partly it is because we have long done things that way. But more important, the habit serves some purpose for us—it appears to get us something. Habits are especially difficult to break because the benefits we think we gain—real or imagined—are valued. The more we seem to gain, the stronger becomes the habit. So much so that you might even say that we grow into the habit of having habits!

For instance, your assistant, Mary, prides herself on being as nice as nice can be—a regular Goody Two Shoes. She always defers to others, never calls her own plays. Instead, she slavishly hews to the oldest maxim in corporate life, the one that says, Go along to get along. Her several promotions appear to affirm its validity. Now, no matter what, her course is always chosen by others. She believes their opinions are more valuable than her own.

Then there's your boss, Jason. He might as well be called Mr. Skeptic. Nothing anyone says meets his needs or delivers what he wants in just the way he wants it. Because of the endless revisions Jason demands, each task he assigns is more like a career than a project.

But the real piece of work is Jason's boss, Delphine. When it comes to taking on responsibility, Delphine just can't say no. As a result, her schedule is so crowded that her 10:00 A.M. meetings rarely begin before 2:00 in the afternoon. If, heaven forbid, you are on her schedule for four o'clock, better call home and tell 'em you're going to be late for supper. Very late.

Mary, Jason, and Delphine are all creatures of habit.

Habit influences Mary to seek safety in the advice of others before making a decision.

A desire within your boss to hit a home run every time is at the center of Jason's habit of micro-managing.

And a need within his boss to get everybody to hurry up and wait only confirms Delphine's habit of appearing indispensable.

So much for resistance to change.

Turn now to the second of five communication spoilers, a phenomenon I call *wandering focus.*

To make you aware of it, I'm going to ask you to try a little experiment. No matter where you are at the moment, in your office, on a plane, take a good look around. Pick an object to focus on. The tray table in front of you, a chair, the telephone, any object at all.

Now, I want you to focus 100 percent on it.

Go on, put the book down. And to the exclusion of all else, concentrate on the object you selected.

Take your time. And when you're done, come on back.

Okay, let me guess what happened. For about five or ten seconds you locked on. Then the trolley jumped the tracks. Your field of attention widened. Your concentration wandered. You brought it back. But it probably wandered again.

The point is, your undivided attention isn't so undivided after all.

If it wanders under controlled circumstances like this, just imagine what goes on when you are engaged in conversation.

Given the phenomenon of wandering focus, how is it you are able to comprehend what others may say to you in conversation? We'll develop the answer in a moment or two. But before we do, there are several observations worth noting.

Most people would rather think their own thoughts than consider yours. In talking with someone else you compete for their attention. It wavers between what you are saying and what they are thinking.

For an example of people operating on different wavelengths

together, take a look at Harlan and Jean. They head up Southern United's task force on the annual workshop conference.

"The last two weeks in July shape up the best, Jean. That's when most accounts slow down. But the problem is, it's also vacation time. So we better make plans ASAP. I got so many Memphis-bashing letters from the field last year I don't think we ought to consider going back there. What about Phoenix?"

Jean thought for a moment. "The last two weeks in July? It's hotter than blazes in Phoenix but I guess that's when the rates drop. I'll have to buy some summer clothes. Nothing in my closet's going to fit me this year."

"A couple of hotels there say they're willing to go the extra mile to get our business. They've all got great golf and from what I hear, the facilities are terrific. I think the division team will really go for Phoenix."

"Do you know how much weight I've put on since the Memphis fiasco?" Jean really wasn't asking. She was telling. "Seven pounds. I've got to start taking it off right now or I'll never be able to show my face on the beach. Remember the conference at the Del Coronado in San Diego a couple of years back? I hope we can get the same block of rooms."

The discussion between Jean and Harlan only looks like a dialogue. It's really a couple of soliloquies.

They aren't listening to each other.

They're tuned to their own preoccupations.

And it is no wonder. After all, when you talk with someone else, your listener is never wholly yours. His attention vacillates between what you are saying and he is thinking.

The third communication spoiler is the phenomenon I call *unwarranted expectations.*

Imagine this scene.

Sales manager Riva Putterwaite calls in one of her district salespeople, Richard Coa, a man who, until the last quarter, consistently led the division. As the present sales period draws to a midpoint, Dick is running 15 percent below budget and 21 percent below target. Riva's concerned. Her intention is to gently uncover the gremlins that might be fouling up her star sales performer. So she says, "Listen, Dick, I'm getting a little tense about the numbers."

Dick, who's going through a nasty divorce, comes to the meeting feeling as though his grip is slipping. Riva's opening gambit adds to his anxiety. What he hears her saying is, "Dick, you're in trouble and you better get on the stick."

What he says, his voice cracking with near-hysteria, is: "For two years straight I've led the division. Don't I deserve more than a chewing out?"

Instead of taking people for all they are really worth we tend to take them for granted. We expect them to know what we mean even though we leave gaps in the information we provide.

Riva assumes Dick understands her good intentions.

Dick assumes Riva knows he is going through emotional hell.

When we make assumptions about what the other person knows, when we feel he or she *ought to know* something, we can expect communication to boomerang. Unless they work from a crystal ball, the audience is almost sure to arrive at conclusions that differ from the ones we intend to get across.

Distrust is the fourth communication spoiler.

Many people—too many, if you ask me—are counseled by an inner caution to conceal their thoughts and feelings. They operate on the Miranda assumption—anything they say will be used against them.

So they clam up.

Say as little as they can get away with.

And in the process, defeat their own best interests.

For an article I wrote recently for one of the in-flight magazines, I needed the views of a younger manager. One of my friends put me on to a fellow working at a major New England insurance company.

Over lunch, I explained what the piece was about. When coffee arrived, I asked him to tell me a little about himself.

Little is exactly what he said. "I've got an MBA from Wayne State University."

Silence.

"And what kind of work do you do now?"

"Portfolio management."

Longer silence.

"Enjoy your work?"

"Yes."

Trying to draw out this fellow was like pulling teeth. Because nothing he said led me to believe it was worth the effort,

I eventually turned away from him and toward the dessert menu (I took solace in the Crème Brûlée).

Several days later I found a likelier candidate. She described herself and her work with evident pleasure.

A couple of months down the road, after the article appeared, she got in touch to say the article was a factor in the terrific annual performance review she had just gotten from her boss.

Psychologists explain habitual secretiveness on the grounds that some people don't like themselves very much. They don't even like their own thoughts and feelings. And they feel if you knew them, you either wouldn't care much for them or you'd try to take advantage of them. It's a dog-chasing-its-tail kind of problem. To avoid rejection, they take shelter in concealment; concealment comes across as distrust; distrust earns rejection.

Lousy listening is the fifth and final communication spoiler.

Business communication depends more on the spoken word than on the written. But here's the problem: The effectiveness of the spoken word hinges not so much on how people talk as on how they listen.

Sure, people have ears and hear well. But they seldom acquire the skills of listening. Never mind that listening is the primary means by which we learn. We listen about three times as much as we read. Still, nobody's really taught how to listen. To be sure, teachers admonish us to pay attention. Drill sergeants warn us to "listen up." But these amount to little more than nets for the wind.

The root cause is a fact so obvious it appears to be an oversimplification and so fundamental to the conduct of our lives it is actually part of the genetic code. To wit: Minds work faster than mouths!

We think much faster than the 100 to 125 words per minute at which we speak. When we listen we are asking our brain to receive words at a rate well below its capacity.

Slowing down our thought processes is, if not wholly impossible, then certainly a very difficult thing to do. So what happens is this: The spoken word arrives at a slow pace while our thoughts continue to race ahead. The differential between thinking and speaking leaves plenty of room for ideas and words to creep in.

As we assemble ideas we inject words of our own—words

and thoughts that are never spoken. We cannot always have what we want when we want it but excess brain capacity doesn't stop us from trying. We interpret facts to create a world of our own making and, given some isolated information, often jump to the wrong conclusion.

When what we hear is different from what is being said, the inability to pace listening to speaking contributes to the difference. So in the end, it is the misuse of spare thinking capacity that really gets in the way of communication.

It amounts to wishful hearing, a phenomenon professors Gail and Michele Myers characterize under the rubric, "How's That Again?":

> I know you believe you understand what you think I said, but I am not sure you realize that what you heard is not what I meant.

Another observer on the effective listening scene spells out the consequences:

A, the boss, is talking to B, the subordinate, about a new program that the firm is planning to launch. B is a poor listener. He has difficulty concentrating on what A has to say. B finds that, because of A's slow rate of speech, he has time to think of things other than the spoken line of thought. He decides to sandwich a few thoughts of his own into the aural ones that are arriving so slowly. So B dashes out onto a mental sidetrack and thinks something like this: "Oh, yes, before I leave I want to tell A about the big success of the meeting I called yesterday." Then B comes back to A's spoken line of thought and listens for a few more words. There is plenty of time for B to dash away and he continues to take sidetracks. But sooner or later, on one of his mental detours, B is almost sure to stay away too long. When he returns, A is moving ahead of him. It becomes harder for B to understand A because he has missed part of the oral message.

Effective verbal communication on the job is nothing more than good conversation—a two-way relationship—dressed up in work clothes. At best the give-and-take, action-and-reaction, yield a pooling of information, a shared interest, or a coming together of views.

Habit, wandering focus, unwarranted expectations, distrust,

lousy listening—these are the five communication spoilers that work against a meeting of the minds.

It's a mistake to think that it's in your power to eradicate them.

What is possible, however, are effective strategic responses. That's what the following chapter is all about.

7

BEFORE YOU UNLEASH STRATEGY

THE CASE FOR SECULAR LOVE

Communication is the engine of empowerment.

By developing the ability to share our thoughts and views, we benefit not merely from the work of others or from greater control over our own business destinies. No, the growth factor we derive is among the most enabling benefits of all—a sense of shared fulfillment.

As managers, we communicate to create our own success. And as leaders, to liberate the success of others—our peers, subordinates, and superiors.

Just as any relationship requires genuine and open communication to stay healthy, so relationships within business organizations improve when ideas are shared honestly and freely. The art lies not in simply being good senders or receivers because the issue is not just the mechanical exchange of data. No matter how clever the expression of your idea, if no one shares it, nothing is gained; if no one cares, all is lost.

Though skills are important, what truly fosters communication comes into play quietly well before the elements of strategic communication make themselves felt. I am talking about an underlying quality that is less a matter of method than of attitude, a compassionate way of thinking and being which aims at a mutual understanding of needs and responsibilities.

Characterized by the words *secular love,* this attitude is for me at the very heart of shared meaning. It bespeaks patience, fairness, and a willingness both to care and to share. Its power emerges from an honest concern for the well-being of the other fellow.

"Love," second only to "free," is the most abused word in the language. It appears to take on a particularly paradoxical aspect in the context of business. In no way do I intend by its use to suggest saccharine sentimentality, spontaneity, possessiveness, romance, or even affection.

Quite the contrary.

For me, secular love is based on the liberating and businesslike idea that caring and liking are not one and the same.

I do not believe any of us likes all of the people who report to us. To greater or lesser degree there are always some individuals we are going to find disagreeable. Nor are we always 100 percent fond of those to whom we report. Yet, if we are to be effective both as managers and leaders, it is necessary and practical to harbor a genuine concern for their well-being. To playact at loving them in an affectionate way, a way that is contrary to our inner feelings, risks backfire. Like the emperor's clothes, the masks we put on, the false cues we give off to the people around us, are all too transparent. Deceptive at first, sooner or later they are seen through—and rejected—by others.

What we can do without compromising our personal values, however, is set out to do good insofar as they are concerned. In this way, secular love permits us to act in genuine and caring ways toward people we may not especially like.

In practice, secular love supports business communication through acceptance of self, acceptance of others, and respect for individuality.

Acceptance of self may seem a curious starting point for a discussion about how to affect and influence our peers, subordinates, and superiors. But it is nevertheless critical. Without it, rising managers often do themselves more harm than good.

Writing the last sentence reminds me instantly of a point early in my career when I was interviewing with New York's Grey Advertising.

Grey then (and, for all I know, still) suffered the reputation of being a hard-driving sweatshop. At first I was untroubled by horror stories of a system that chewed up creative types with all the compassion of a mill grinding corn. After all, when it came to the expenditure of energy, I could show hummingbirds a thing or two. I got a kick out of working hard and doing well, and the rewards Grey was talking about amounted to more than pocket change.

Still, as the interview process escalated, my internal radar picked up signals to the contrary. Notwithstanding the prospect of nearly doubling my salary, I found myself growing leery. Everybody I had talked with outside the agency spoke of a real Simon Legree atmosphere. But, to a man, the Grey eminences pooh-poohed my doubts. The next-to-last interviewer suggested that all my suspicions would be allayed once I met one of the high muckety-mucks—a guy named Dick Lessler. Lessler, he reported, was living proof that at Grey, the quality of opportunity and the quality of life were in sync.

For a reason that will become clear in just a second, it was obvious from the get-go that Lessler's reassurance lacked resonance. He was hiding part of himself. Not just from me but from himself. Behind a facade of passion intended to pass for honesty, he talked about the deep and abiding respect he had for the people on his team. "Spinal respect" is the curious way he put it.

I wondered who he was kidding more, me or himself?

How he could think he was really succeeding was beyond me, for there, on the wall immediately behind his desk, was the telltale. It was irrefutable evidence that communicated his inability to accept his own drive—some might even say, hucksterism. It was a pair of elaborately framed spurs, the most lethal I had ever laid eyes on.

I guess Lessler found my demurral too off-putting because, in the end, Grey never made an offer. Perhaps the loss was mine. I think not entirely so. Others from whose talent Grey might have benefited more than mine could not help but see what I saw.

To increase self-acceptance is not a matter of reading books like the one in your hands now. It is a matter of reading yourself—understanding who you really are instead of trying to present yourself as what you are not.

The more you pretend, the more you tend to buy into your own myth and, therein, lose touch with reality, yours and that of the world around you.

Just as caring and liking are not one and the same, so it is with acceptance and approval: Under the umbrella of secular love, you can communicate with others whose behavior and outlook don't correspond to yours without having to agree with them or even condone their behavior.

How we experience the world is in some ways unique and in others a shared experience. Although we can never really be certain our perceptions are the same as the next fellow's, it is only human to think so. As a consequence, we tend to want to reject others when they represent ideas contrary to ours. Deep down inside, we are unsettled by the discovery that the values and outlook of people with whom we are in business contact do not correspond to the ones we hold. Their disagreement makes us uncomfortable because it forces us to reexamine our position, question our views, and confront our beliefs.

Depending on who challenges us and whether we consider their values particularly important, these conflicts can provoke anxiety. To resolve them means to engage in what we ordinarily perceive to be a win-lose situation. None of us likes to lose. And even if we emerge the so-called winner, we know from experience that losers never forget, and may be willing to wait a long time to get even.

The remedy for the anxiety this power game provokes lies in a nonjudgmental attitude, one that opens the way to a win-win option.

The idea is to separate people from their behavior so as to be able to accept the person *despite* the conflict.

Acceptance—the ability to separate behaviors from their sources—reflects a view of business communication in which right and wrong are largely irrelevant.

Neutrality is useful because the essence of communication is sharing. So long as you conduct yourself in a way that is judgmental—in a zero-sum way that produces winners and losers—you will inevitably find yourself diminishing others to make more of yourself. The effect is to alienate yourself from the people you mean to reach. When you are by yourself you cannot share.

Impotent communicators need and want concurrence. In fact, they cannot function without it. So they seek out and reward points of view that coincide with their own and punish those that differ.

Meanwhile, the effective business communicator knows that the truly important thing is not to agree so much as it is to disagree without disengaging.

That is the true meaning of acceptance.

Having seen two of the three ways secular love supports

communication—through acceptance of self and through acceptance of others—we'll complete the triangle by turning now to the third leg, respect for the other guy.

Toward the midpoint of a recent professional basketball season, the New York Knicks seemed to collapse right before fans' eyes. "I've seen a lot of things but I've never really seen a professional team fall apart," said Maurice Cheeks, the starting point guard in his twelfth league season. "When you're losing, guys get frustrated. That's when you're tested. We don't have to love each other. But we have to work together and respect each other."

Respect is a one-word handle for the complex process that allows and encourages the other fellow to be the other fellow and not a carbon copy of ourselves. It bespeaks an ability on our part to refrain from domination, from the imposition of our own values.

It empowers others by recognizing their individuality, self-direction, and their right to self-determination—up to and including their right to be wrong.

Respect, in other words, is the reverse of mistrust.

It invites people to be forthright and forthcoming. At the same time, it assuages fears they may harbor that we will barge past the opening they provide to overwhelm their independence and reduce them to dependency.

Respect benefits both sides of the business communication equation.

By contributing to an environment for success in which others are encouraged to explore the outer limits of their talent, ability, and ambition, respect nurtures a spirit of independence. To the degree their prowess grows as a result, the respect we receive in return releases us from the onerous and burdensome feeling that we are somehow responsible for their performance on the job.

Early on in our careers, we learn that being ourselves opens us to certain risks. As immature fledglings, we figure that the best thing that can happen to us in a business situation is that we prevail. Unfortunately, what takes more time to learn is that winning isn't all it is cracked up to be. We discover that, as in every win-lose proposition, there's a price—the risk of alienating others, making enemies, and finding ourselves alone.

Most of us eventually achieve sufficient business maturity to free ourselves from the win-lose mentality.

Others, unfortunately, remain victimized by it. In response to the stresses provoked by the fear of losing, many of these people disengage entirely, moving instead toward dependency, a state of being in which they take no decision on their own, hence assume no risk of giving offense.

For living proof of dependency as a way of business life, I want to call your attention once again to your assistant, Mary. You remember her. She's the woman we mentioned in the last chapter. The one whose habit is to rely entirely on the opinion of others.

Mary's behavior seems at first a paradigm of innocuous innocence, but it has its dark side.

Let me explain.

Her habit of getting others to do for her the things she needs to do for herself puts them in the unhappy position of being the instruments of her enfeeblement. The response she asks for actually reinforces the impression in their minds and in hers that she is somehow fragile, crippled, or otherwise disempowered.

Like the curious phenomenon of the Americans held hostage in Iran who found themselves identifying with their oppressors, Mary identifies most closely with those whose lack of respect renders her powerless. Instead of contributing to her self-esteem, their so-called help further violates her self-worth. That leaves her with feelings she'd rather not communicate.

For Mary, it is a pernicious and self-fulfilling cycle: The more she relies on the business views of others, the less empowered she feels. The less empowered she feels, the more she relies on others.

Unchecked, her dependency, hence her inability to really communicate, has a half-life of forever.

If dependency's the poison, respect is the antidote.

Within the embrace of secular love, respect for Mary constrains you to carefully avoid the so-called help that diminishes her strength, resourcefulness, and self-esteem. As her boss, you respect her by regarding her as capable of fulfilling her aspirations. You let her know in a kind way that you expect her to be productive on her own.

Remember, the object of respect is not to absorb other people in your individuality. It is to celebrate theirs. By separating people from the dependencies they create, you more than support acceptance of your thinking. You encourage them to share their own.

Having come to the end of this chapter, I am left in a binary, yes-no mental state. It goes like this:

We get the kind of communication we deserve.

To the degree we sacrifice human values for the sake of a mechanistic exchange of data, it renders both sides impotent.

On the other hand, by approaching it in the spirit of secular love, the process reveals as much about the people involved as it does anything else—who we are, what we expect from ourselves and each other, and what it is like to work together—and creates for each of us an opportunity for mutual fulfillment.

Now, while the concept is fresh in your mind, I'd like you to do us both a favor. Take a look at the next chapter. It sets the strategy for leveraging secular love one-on-one, getting the other guy to really open up to your thinking.

8

PHYSICAL LISTENING

THE ZEN OF SENDING IS RECEIVING

Despite the absence of a surefire formula, several decades of practical on-the-job experience convince me that getting the minds of others to attend our views begins with self-acceptance, acceptance of others, and with respect for their individuality. These, the three constituents of secular love we discussed in the last chapter, do not create communication. What they establish are *the conditions that permit communication to occur.*

By invoking these elements we make evident to our contacts that we do not intend to diminish them in the process of making our ideas their ideas. Rather, we seek to establish through secular love a platform of common ground between us. A bridge to support shared thought.

The very idea suggests connectedness. Oneness. An environment for mutual success in which the goals of the communicator and the goals of the audience are, if not the same, then certainly in harmony.

To implement secular love, to get others to really open up to our thinking, entails the ability to *listen,* to *deal with emotions,* and to *feed back* responses. Only then, when the ground has been prepared properly, are we in position to rivet attention on content through the principles of *strategic communication.*

For the rest of this chapter we're going to examine the topic of listening—not why we don't (which we looked at a couple of chapters back under the rubric, *Lousy Listening*) but how we can improve our ability to receive and digest the signals transmitted by others.

Let's agree that the first step is to understand what gets in the way.

As somewhat inadequate human beings, with all the faults, foibles, and fears that implies, each of us practices *selective listening.*

There are things we like and things we do not. Ideas we are afraid of and thoughts we're ashamed to own up to. Words we like to hear and things that are so off-putting we go out of our way to avoid them. The net of it is that we tune out what we do not want to hear in order to attend better to what we agree with.

When we neither agree nor wish to agree with a speaker's argument, most of us hear the first few words or sentences all right. Get the drift of what the speaker is saying. Decide it is not for us. And bingo!—either interrupt right then and there or turn our inner attention to prepare a mental rebuttal.

It was said of the famous communication maven, Marshall McLuhan, that he was too polite to interrupt speakers he disagreed with—in his case, most of the rest of the world. "He always waits," one scathing interviewer wrote, "until the other person's lips quit moving."

An evolutionary phenomenon explains our response to ideas with which we disagree. I'm talking about the fight-or-flight mechanism. This vestigial system conditions us to treat the threat of disagreement as an all or nothing proposition. When it senses the possibility of victory, it directs us to stubbornly stand our ground, and when hegemony is not possible, drives us to flee so that we may conserve our energy to fight under more favorable conditions.

When saber-toothed tigers preyed the land and fearsome sharks the sea, fight-or-flight was the difference between extinction and a future. But in today's modern business era, when tigers are cheered as go-getters and sharks are the people you lunch with, it seems an especially primitive and counterproductive adaptation. It works against our evolution as rising managers. The more we give in to fight-or-flight urges, the less able we are to take care of business in the calm, collected ways that best serve our agendas, needs, and interests.

The more evolved and human response to dealing with disagreeable ideas is through the cluster of communication skills called effective listening.

These work two ways.

First, by enabling us to capture the critical content of spoken statements in order to assess situations more accurately, they lend fresh credence to the age-old business belief that superior knowledge is power.

Second, they lead others to see us as the kind of person who not only grasps what is said but who understands and considers—but does not necessarily agree with—what others have to offer.

At the heart of effective listening lie four constellations of skills. These are the abilities to *attend,* to *respond,* to *seek more information,* and to *value silence.* Before we go into them, let's see them in action. What we'll do first is catch a bird's eye view, then, moving forward, expand on selected situations step-by-step.

If I have to eat another piece of skinless broiled chicken, Letitia Brookenson thought, *I'll sprout feathers.*

For what seemed like an eon she stood there, transfixed by the cafeteria's menu board. The thought crossed her mind that she had never before realized how many different ways there are to spell b-o-r-i-n-g.

"Tish, I *must* speak with you!"

A shout arose behind her. The up-and-down quality struck a familiar note of anguish. She turned. Half-a-dozen places behind her in the line, Ben Durfee gesticulated. Ben Durfee also shouted. "That task force meeting . . ." he was saying.

Ben operated as though every time he opened his mouth history was in the making.

As she stepped out of the line to walk toward him, she wondered if Ben realized that when everything is urgent nothing can be.

Approaching him, Tish was careful to take a spot neither so far from him it would encourage more shouting nor so close as to be uncomfortable.

As they moved with the line, Tish listened carefully to what Ben had to say, leaning toward him and nodding.

They took a table. He continued to hold court.

From time to time, she spoke.

Half an hour later, a glazed look crossed her eyes. It was a momentary thing. Coming out of it, she cocked her head to say, "I'm a little lost, Ben. Would you mind running that by me again?"

He repeated himself.

Toward the end of lunch, after a lull in the conversation

during which she savored the flavor of fresh-brewed coffee, Tish said, "Is there anything else on your mind, Ben?"

"I think that about wraps it up for now, Tish. Thanks."

Because she is an accomplished listener, Tish brings to bear the four sets of skills involved in effective listening. We'll go through them one-by-one, beginning with the first cluster, *attending.*

The big idea here is the concept of *physical listening.* It's premised on the certain knowledge that it is never enough just to listen.

You must be *perceived* as listening!

Approach the other fellow, cock your head, lean forward, make and sustain eye contact—you name it! When you listen in a physical way, all kinds of good things go on at once. Those of a Zen persuasion might think of it as sending by receiving. To a more Western outlook, it's unmistakable evidence of respect for and acceptance of the other person. It shows you think he or she is worth your attention in the first place.

In more than one way, Tish revealed her intent to be there for Ben. First, she used her feet before she used her ears—she moved closer. Then she positioned herself at an appropriate distance, roughly three feet. Too much air between them leads people to feel anxiety over the need to be heard. They signal their discomfort by raising their voices. On the other hand, when speaker and audience are too close anxieties also rise, this time because things seem more confrontational.

The distance between yourself and another person that supports communication best is a matter of trial and error. Seated or standing, three feet seems about right for most people in our culture. Watch for signs of anxiety: raised voice, fidgeting, shifting from one foot to the other, avoiding eye contact. Position yourself accordingly.

The second cluster of skills Tish brought to bear were the ones categorized under the ability to *respond.*

Like hearts that pump unprompted and lungs that breathe with no conscious thought, many of the skills of responding are involuntary. For instance, at one point in their conversation, Tish turned to Ben.

"Let me have that phone number," she said.

"569-1312," Ben replied.

"569-1312?"

"You got it!"

Repeating the number is an act of affirmation—Tish confirmed the information Ben transmitted. But even more important is the atmosphere Tish creates by playing back the number. It signals in yet another way her presence in the conversation. Between the lines, Tish transmits her understanding of the difference between being in a conversation because one has to and being involved because one wants to. She tells him that she actively *chooses* to take part.

The key to making effective responses lies in the skill of restating, in your own words, the information you are receiving. When the senders agree with your understanding they are encouraged to continue. On the other hand, if they disagree with your playback, it is incumbent on them to clarify things by explaining the point in a fresh or different way or by adding new information.

Here's how it went between Tish and Ben:

"Ben, I'd like us both to be clear on this," Tish said as they reached their table. "You are telling me the concept is on target but the money's a bit much."

Ben set his tray down. "Well not exactly, Tish. The money thing is not insurmountable. I could sell my boss. But to tell you the truth, I am not convinced this is an issue we can simply throw money at and abracadabra!—it's gone."

As she listened, Tish mentally took apart Ben's flow of thoughts. She separated the main point he was making from the minor ones.

"The goal here," Ben was saying, "is to get all twelve of them in on the program." Ben spoke between morsels. At first, he paid more attention to his food than to her. Several moments later, he put down his knife and fork. "I mean, nine of them in the Eastern Division can be Ames's baby. He's got the kind of clout we need for this one." A thoughtful look crossed Ben's face. "I remember what he did in the last seminar we put on. But the truth is, Tish, the economy's a whole lot tighter now. Still, Ames gets my vote. If anybody can bring all twelve aboard, he can." Ben looked directly into Tish's eyes. His voice dropped an octave. "We need the dozen," he said, "the whole dozen, and nothing but the dozen."

As he spoke, Ben made it easy for Tish to distinguish his main point from the minor ones. For one thing, he repeated it several times. And for another, he lent an added dimension of drama to his main verbal thrust. Together, these created an unmistakable tonality that helped Tish interpret Ben's words correctly.

"Let me see if I can summarize, Ben," Tish responded. "If we don't get all twelve we can't get to critical mass."

As the conversation continued through the main course, Tish felt her strength drain. And with good reason. After all, effective listening takes real concentration. Inevitably, though, waning energy begets wandering attention.

It was only a momentary lapse but by the time she was able to refocus on Ben's words, it was too late. She had missed too big a chunk of what he had been saying to grasp his meaning.

In a word, she was lost.

As if to underscore the point he was making, Ben narrowed his eyes. An ominous and deliberate edge crept into his voice. "It scares me," he said, "to think what might happen then."

At the sight of the seriousness that played across Ben's face, Tish realized she had allowed her mind to wander. Numbers? Dates? Places? Names? *For goodness sake,* Tish thought, *what did I miss?* She cocked her head. "I'm a little lost, Ben," she said. "Would you mind running that by me again?"

It has been my observation, and probably yours, too, that businesspeople tend to play things close to the vest. But I have had the good fortune to observe also that, human nature being what it is and given an atmosphere of mutual respect, rising managers really prefer to express themselves fully.

The problem is, they don't always know how to open up, how to share.

Effective listener that she is, Tish brought into play the skill of *seeking more information.* Through it, she worked to give Ben the room to talk about things as he saw and felt them.

Going into the conversation Tish knew that Ben, like most

everybody else, was of two minds. On the one hand, part of him wanted to respond to her expressions of interest. Pushing back against that was a natural feeling of secretiveness. The less Tish knew about his views the better off he might be in the long run.

Without interrupting the flow of talk or breaking the mood, Tish sought to encourage Ben to open up in ways that let him know she was listening. True, she wanted to do it in a manner that stayed out of Ben's way. But she didn't want to be so distant as to lead Ben to think she was not participating.

As Ben talked, Tish made simple responses that signaled her participation and encouraged him to continue. These were sprinkled throughout the conversation—sometimes in words, other times in tone of voice or facial expression, occasionally with all three.

A look of genuine anguish came over Ben's face. His fingers fidgeted with the napkin he had placed beside his plate. "I'm so darn wrapped up in this project I can't see the forest for the trees anymore," he said. "Talking about it makes it seem even more of a lose-lose proposition."

Tish considered her options in a trice. She could keep her own counsel, but that left Ben dangling. It was plain that he *wanted* encouragement.

Okay. She could jump in with a generous helping of good advice. But Tish knew in her heart that Ben was looking for his own way out of the bind.

Or she could find an unobtrusive way to let Ben know she was with him all the way as he searched for his own answers.

"Lose-lose proposition," she said, her brow a-furrow.

Repeating the speaker's last thought.

Amplifying it with an appropriate facial expression.

That's all it took for Tish to communicate empathy. It gave Ben the feeling she understood what was going on with him. Even more important, told him she was not judging him.

He felt safe continuing. "That's it, Tish, unless I can figure out a way to take care of the people in manufacturing. Wait a New York minute here! Suppose, I mean just suppose, I went to Jordan and let him know what's what. Hmmm. I think maybe that's the way to go!"

"Uh-huh."
"I see."

"Right."

"Go on."

The words you choose to encourage others to speak more fully are less important than the intent you mean to convey. Any way you phrase it, the deeper message needs to be, "Please continue."

But sometimes it takes more than a minimalist approach to draw out other people. There are moments when a skillfully put question might be a good thing. But as with most other aspects of communication, the line between boon and bane is thin.

Think for a moment of the best nonbusiness book you've read in the last year or so. Chances are, the reason you liked it so well was that the dialogue seduced you. Realistic people saying things in ways that seem genuine. Now think of the worst piece of fiction you've read recently. I daresay the reason it underwhelmed you had also to do with the dialogue. Only in this case, the words probably rang false. I suspect that if you were to return to the more forgettable of the two books, you'd discover the author relied too heavily on questions to develop characters and advance the plot.

Just as you as a reader grow tired of a litany of questions, so too do others whom you might inadvertently interrogate. Peppering others with question after question creates a feeling that, instead of participating in give-and-take, you are conducting a cross-examination. After a while, each question is experienced as an irritation. What escalates most, of course, is resentment. And when that happens, it's goodbye communication!

Rationalizing questions on the grounds that you seek to help another to more fully express his or her thoughts and feelings won't wash. Barrages of questions don't facilitate communication. They bespeak the questioner's attempt to dictate the direction of the conversation rather than allowing others to explore the situation in a more self-directed way.

Before you ask question number one, it is well to bear in mind the purpose of encouragement in the first place. It is to center the conversation on the concerns of the other, not to provide you with information. Besides, to the degree you keep asking questions, it figures that you've got to take the time to dream up those questions. That's an almost certain formula for listening failure: The time you take to formulate questions is time you cannot spend focusing on what the other guy has to say.

"I happened to mention it to Davis Breen over in HR," Ben was saying. "The very thought seemed to make him uncomfortable. He said there was no point trying to buck the head-count policy." Ben looked away.

"Policy."

"That's right." Ben fidgeted.

It seemed to Tish he had reached a point where he wanted help to carry his train of thought forward. "What do you think about the policy?"

Trish's question illuminates the way to formulate queries that truly advance understanding. Namely, ask one that cannot be answered yes or no. Notice that Trish didn't ask if Ben liked the policy. She asked what he thought about the policy. She could have said, with equal effect, "How about the policy?" Or structured her question around Ben's last thought by saying, "Where does head count figure in this?"

The first three of the four listening skills Tish practiced enabled her to attend, to respond, and to draw out Ben. But it was through the fourth skill she brought to bear, the ability to *listen in silence,* that Tish came to understand him.

To arrive at understanding through effective listening is to make contact at two levels simultaneously. The first of these, the fact level, comprises the words the speaker enunciates. The second, the level of emotion, consists of what is unspoken, the *silent* material between the lines that signals the other's *feeling.*

In my experience, more business listeners fail because they fear silence than for almost any other reason you can name. And with good reason, I suppose. Listening between the lines—allowing silence to be—can be discomforting. Even a few seconds devoid of words make some people ill at ease. They have a strong compulsion to break the quiet with questions, advice, sounds, anything! These, of course, prevent the unspoken mood of the conversation from making itself felt in both minds.

One of the reasons people fear silence is that they do not know what to do during the conversational lull. Tish, on the other hand, had learned to use the time silence provides both to continue to demonstrate physical listening and to think about what had gone down.

Toward the end of lunch, during that lull in the conversation when she savored the flavor of the fresh-brewed coffee, Tish thought about what Ben had said. She wondered how she would feel and what she would think if she were in Ben's shoes. And what she concluded was that for all of their differences in personality and outlook, she and Ben were probably more alike than different in some respects. His concerns were understandable. No wonder he was worried. The chances were, they weren't going to find the solution instantly. It would take time. Meanwhile, she could help Ben reach temporary closure—to feel that he had taken the thing as far as he could for the nonce.

After a few quiet moments she said, "Is there anything else on your mind, Ben?"

"I think that about wraps it up for now, Tish. Thanks."

Through appropriate silence—excessive silence can be as much of a turnoff as too much talking—Tish gave Ben the opportunity to consider what he had said and what remained to be done.

Effective listening isn't passive.

It communicates actively. It tells others they are worth time, attention, and focus.

Nor is it purely mental.

Actually, it is a physical act. An involved and involving opportunity to exercise our humanity through giving and taking.

Psychotherapist Carl Rogers believes effective listening reflects a willing orientation to life and to people. He says that to listen is to have the creative power to imagine how it would make sense to say what the other person is saying.

What Rogers does not say is that effective listening is easy because it is not. Nobody's a born listener. It takes conscious effort. But short of an IQ that's so low it requires you to be watered twice a day, you can be certain that when you do the hard work of listening in a thoughtful and deliberate way, listening works!

Effective listening is the first of two ways to leverage the power of secular love.

The second—dealing with emotion and feedback—begins on page 66.

9

DEALING WITH EMOTION

RESIST RESISTING RESISTANCE

In the last chapter we learned that to leverage secular love, to get others to really open up to us, two sets of skills need to come on-line. We concentrated on the first of these—the ability to listen. Now the time has come to examine the second—the ability to deal with emotion.

There's usually a good reason to think that facts make communication happen but there's almost always a better reason to think they do not. It is what happens to facts, how we process them internally, that determines our ability to persuade, inspire, and inform others.

There's just one thing facts do. They trigger emotions. In the end, pride, anger, fear, guilt, shame, envy, and joy—the primal feelings—are the true motivators. I'll demonstrate several proofs of that statement in a moment. But first, consider the implications of what General H. Norman Schwarzkopf, the United States commander in the Persian Gulf, has to say on the subject of emotion. "Fear," he points out, "is a great thing. In battle, it makes you do things smart instead of dumb."

As the general's remark suggests, emotions are more than the personal baggage each of us schleps through life. They are the kaleidoscope through which we view and respond to the world.

We can no more leave our feelings at home on the doorstep when we head for the office in the morning than abandon our eyesight. Yet, in the traditional view of commerce, we're supposed to keep blinders on emotion. This leads us to block their direct expression, but, since feelings really can't be contained, we experience the blockage as tension.

Now when tension strikes, the natural inclination is to get rid of the strain. So to help us cope, we force the emotions out one way or another.

Take the tension salespeople experience when they come up against an objection. It often stimulates the drive they need to break through resistance.

Deena Havens was giving Seamus Kahane a tough time. He was a new salesman. And though he represented a conservative, old-line envelope company she had done business with for years, her last experience with the previous salesperson had soured her. At first, Seamus didn't mind taking heat. After a while, though, her complaints began to sound picky, picky, picky! Still, when he thought the time was right, he asked for the order.

"How do you expect me to give you an order when the last guy messed me up on delivery?" she barked back. "You're probably as disorganized as the rest of them."

Kahane felt his Irish climb. Dammit! Nothing was going to shame him out of this account and embarrass him with his boss, not even the customer!

"Ms. Havens, let's be honest," Seamus said. "Envelopes aren't exactly rocket science. You are a hundred percent right: the real difference between us and our competition is service. If you'll give me a test order I'll get my boss to okay twice the quantity. That way, the next time you are ready, we can resupply overnight—and that's a guarantee!"

If tension is one end of the emotional continuum that provokes action, the feelings underlying joy are another.

Assistant Design Manager—oops, make that Design Manager—Herb Voorhees couldn't wait to get out on the exercise floor. An hour earlier his boss broke the news. The competition was over. Herb got the promotion he had been bucking for. The announcement would be made to the organization in a week or so. Meanwhile, they asked him to keep the news under wraps. Under wraps? He felt like one of the vultures in the cartoon on the wall in the boss's office—the one that was saying, "Patience, my ass! If something doesn't happen soon I'm going to have to kill somebody." About to burst and ready to mount his treadmill, Herb knew today would be the day to break his personal best. So he punched up the speed to ten miles an hour, jumped aboard, and quickly lost himself in longer, smoother strides than any he had known before.

Because a seam of emotional coal runs through the geology of most business communication, guilt burns through banked fires of self-criticism, confessions of real or imagined misdeeds, and acts of atonement. Anger, on the other hand, smolders in argument, gossip, destructive criticism, teasing, or lack of cooperation.

This process of displacement, by which rising managers relieve emotions indirectly, goes a long way toward explaining two of the great conundrums of human business development: First, how ordinary people sometimes deliver the most extraordinary business results; and second, why some of our most promising managers occasionally produce some of the worst.

Let's suppose that, due to a budget cut, Jennifer loses her assistant. Ordinarily that hardly merits comment. But Jennifer's case is rather special. She has a phone phobia. Only she doesn't know it. Every time she has to ring up a stranger, her heart races a mile a minute. Her voice gets wimpy. She comes off ineffective. Here's the kicker: Her career with the March of Dimes now depends on aggressively booking celebrities for photo sessions with the poster child. Until a month or so ago, Jennifer's assistant made those calls. Now, Jennifer refuses to take the blame for the recent string of strikeouts. With her world-weary sarcasm, she rationalizes a case: stars are rats spelled backwards. And everybody knows the rats' agents are the biggest vermin of all.

As the deadline approaches, her boss, Alana-Beth, tries to dispel the problem. "It's like fishing," Alana-Beth advises. "The more lines you get out, the better your chances of landing a big one. Just keep on trying." Her rationale is unavailing. Jennifer is frozen in place, unable to connect.

The scenario epitomizes the hand-and-glove problems raised by emotions in the workplace. Jennifer was blind *to* her true feelings; Alana-Beth was blinded *by* them. Between them, neither was able to create the mutual understanding that is the heart of communication on the job.

Though the failure of logic came as something of a shock to Alana-Beth, the outcome was hardly surprising. Her advice to keep everlastingly at it did not address the underlying source of emotional tension—Jennifer's fear of her own inadequacy; it spoke, instead, to the superficial reality—the difficulties of dealing with stars' agents.

The point to be taken is that emotions are not responsive to advice, reason, or logic, all of which exacerbate tension.

Advice often turns out to be criticism in drag, a fig leaf, a social veneer meant to mask the merciless way we sometimes treat one another.

What is the point of telling people the illogic of being illogically scared or angry or anxious? They can't help it. Imagine that you are afraid to fly. Your boss means to encourage you by showing he cares. "If you can't travel," he reasons, basking in watchful concern, "you'll never get the kind of exposure you need out in the field organization." Correct me if I'm wrong but the way I see it, his words are certain to make you not less but more fearful. You are still scared to fly. What is now even worse, you suddenly have the added dread of ending up a potential failure. If reasoning of this sort is an act of kindness, God save us from those who profess to care.

When we are caught up in emotions, admonitions magnify the tension and make it more acute. When I have a feeling, the tension it produces makes me feel I have to act it out. Sometimes the acting out is inappropriate so I sit on the emotion. That makes things all the more tense. For relief, I confide in a colleague. And they say, "Hey, Burt, you shouldn't feel that way."

Hearing that makes me scared. Scared that there's something wrong with me for having the feeling in the first place. And scared that the feeling might overwhelm me and get out of hand.

If my coworkers said they could understand my feelings, understand why I might feel the way I do, I'd be a whole lot better off. At the very least, I'd feel there was nothing wrong with me.

Here's the thing: Telling people you understand their feelings—the first of three ways we will explore to dispel emotion—does not mean you agree with them. It merely says that there is nothing wrong with their feelings.

Emotions are like shadows. In the dim and foreboding light of fear, the issues they reflect loom large. Seen in the friendlier glow of understanding, they assume their truer proportions.

So, to put first things first, *you begin to invoke secular love in an emotional situation by simply encouraging people to ventilate their feelings. You accept, but do not necessarily agree with, their emotions without proscription or prescription.*

The insistent ring of the phone finally roused process safety specialist Dennis Saunders. The giant number 12 storage tank— the one holding the most hazardous material on the site—had developed a bad valve. Dennis's wife, Georgine, wasn't the silent type. "How come you're always the patsy?" she said as he dressed. Her voice dripped scorn. "I thought you said you had seniority!"

By the time he got to the site, Saunders had worked himself into a tizzy. There, he confronted his boss. "Look, I don't wanna sound paranoid or anything but every time a midnight special comes up, it seems like Dennis gets the call. Once in a while? Sure! But enough's enough. I'm fed up!"

The supervisor had a choice. He could make it a win-lose proposition by simply proving to Dennis that he got about as many night calls as anybody else on the team. But in the process of winning the skirmish he'd lose the battle for Dennis's loyalty. On the other hand, by finding a way to help Dennis blow off steam, he'd appear to lose the skirmish but, in the end, win Dennis over. He chose to win by losing.

"I get the feeling, Dennis, you think I am picking on you."

"Yes and no," Dennis responded. "I mean, I know the others get called but it seems like all the worst ones come to me."

The second principle of dealing with emotion through secular love is to encourage further expression. It gets rid of more tension, making acting out less likely. At times, all of us have known anger. By allowing these feelings to air not only do we inflict no harm, we do a lot of good. If the idea of experiencing someone else's angry feelings frightens you, try to remember there is a difference between angry feelings and angry acts.

Having encouraged them to ventilate their feelings and showed them you accept their right to feel as they do, now is the time to *find a way to make them aware of their emotional state.*

Since they are likely to experience a diagnosis as a frontal assault—and quite rightly so—you are better off to suggest the impact of their emotions on you, how it makes you feel. This gives them a handle on the consequences of their behavior and an opportunity to clarify the situation. If they are truly angry, it's an invitation to say why; and if they are not, an invitation to explore whatever the real impediment might be.

"Dennis," the supervisor responded, "it sounds to me like there's more to it than a question of who is on call. If there's some way I've caused you to have this other problem I wish you'd let me in on it to see if we can't set things right. After all, you are the most experienced guy on the safety team and what you think is important to this group."

Dennis thought a moment. "Well, to tell you the truth I am not really angry with you over schedule rotation. I know that's the way the ball bounces and I can live with it. But I'm afraid my wife can't. You see, after these last couple of calls in the middle of the night Georgine's on my case something fierce. She says you guys are taking rotten advantage."

Reality checking is the fourth step in the process of dealing with emotion. It enables you to compare what you hear with what is intended; what they receive with what you transmit. It empowers both sides to sort the true meaning of the communication—emotion as well as content—from the side issues.

The clarifying technique by which both parties check reality is the give-and-take of *feedback.* Every so often, each side describes in its own words the mental image generated by what the other person says. Since the object here is to get beyond words to arrive at meaning

1. *Focus on behavior, not on personality.* The idea is to communicate about what, not about who.
2. *Deal with what is going on between you now, not what went on or will go on.*
3. *Confine your remarks to observations, not interpretations.*
4. *Share information rather than advice.*

"I can understand why she might feel like that, Dennis. But am I getting you correctly? The rotation is okay the way it is?"

Dennis thought for a moment. "Well, not really. I think it might be to everybody's advantage to work out an on-call system so that we know that on certain nights it's going to be my turn and other nights it's yours. I'd feel better and it'd do something for my family life, too."

"Okay, maybe a better rotation can be worked out. Tell you

what, why don't you get right on it. Give it your full attention."

"You mean drop everything else?"

"Well, come to think of it, we've got to get that valve on number 12 recertified. Tell you what, I'll get you some help so that both projects get the attention they need."

Now it is all very nice to say that emotions are defused by the skills associated with secular love. And the fact is, most of the time, they are.

But what happens when you apply those skills and get no place fast? What happens when encouraging people to ventilate, helping them become aware of their emotions, and checking reality through feedback lay a great big egg?

Though it is only natural to resist the other person's refractory emotion, the most important thing to remember when nothing seems to work is to *resist resisting resistance.*

We think of our resistance as natural but, really, it is an educated incapacity—a void in our store of skills that results from our training. Early on we are taught to examine and weigh the merits of arguments. In the process, we learn to resist what we assume to be the inferior case. After all, we can't let their ideas become our ideas when they don't make sense. Unfortunately, an if-it-is-not-right-then-it-must-be-wrong mentality spills over into matters emotional. We treat what we take to be refractory feelings in the same cut-and-dried way we treat facts. We compare them to our own, judge them, and when we determine them to be inferior, we resist, resist, resist!

When you find yourself on the cusp of resistance, you can take several steps to turn the situation around.

First, *accept the emotion and express understanding for it.*

Q. C. lab supervisor Digger Brisbane was in one of his moods. There was no use trying to get any work done on the presentation that was scheduled for the following Monday.

As far as D. B. was concerned, nothing was right! Nothing had ever been right! And if you really want the truth, the whole truth, and nothing but the truth, nothing would ever be right again! If he had a theme song, it was Mick Jagger doing the Stones' tune, the one that went, "I can't get no sat-iss-fack-shun."

"I can appreciate your being anxious, Digger, but hell's bells, man. It's only a job review and you've only had the best year of your career," said John Banner, the department's number two. "I know a lot rides on it, though, and I can see where if I were in your shoes, me boy-o, I might get a little antsy as well."

"Easy for you to say." Digger toyed with a pencil.

Having accepted Brisbane's emotional rigidity, *step two is to feed back the kind of impression the other person's making.*

"Listen, Digger, I don't have nearly the experience you've got but I do know the old man is a fair person. I mean, sure—he's got a short fuse but it doesn't go off all that often and when it does, it's for cause. What I'm telling you is that anxiety's a whole lot worse than the thing itself."

Once you have fed back, a moment of silence is in order. This gives the other a chance to think about what you have said, compare it with what is on his mind, and make a response. Don't be surprised if he offers an excuse, attacks or, what is worse, remains remote. In that event, just recycle to the feedback mode as often as it takes to make a breakthrough.

"Digger, we've been at this for the better part of thirty minutes and I've tried my best. But you don't seem very willing to talk about your feelings. I wonder—is this conversation making you uncomfortable or what?"

"It is," he said at last. "I'm forty-two years old and I've worked for this company for twenty of them. My kid goes off to college in two years and I'm scared because I still don't have enough saved to pay the four years of tuition I promised him. At my age, if I get caught in a squeeze, I'll need the money we've saved so far just to stay afloat."

The point of this chapter is not to make Sigmund Freuds of us all but to make each of us a little better at experiencing the humanity of business.

The authoritarian managers-know-it-all-employees-do-it-all mentality of our fathers in commerce and their fathers before them is, if not dead, then surely moribund.

In the 1990s and beyond, empowerment appears increasingly likely to drive the growth of large organizations. Hegemony will no longer be determined solely by dominant position or hollow prestige. As never before, leadership will be seen as the art of winning and holding the consent of the led. That being the case, rising managers will find the ability to communicate taking on ever-increasing gravity.

Inherent in the ability to persuade, inform, and inspire others will be the understanding we are able to bring to the emotional component of communication.

Emotions are both torment and comfort, attraction and despair, symptoms of and solutions for the solitary tensions that are within us all. They endow our lives with meanings we cannot fully explain. Pain us, please us, warn us, propel us. They raise more questions than they answer and because they do, remind us that our ability to deal with them comes not solely from within ourselves but arises at least in part from our ability to communicate personally with our peers, subordinates, and superiors.

THE WRITTEN WORD

PART III

10

FOOLPROOF WRITING

Forget the old categories.

There are really just two kinds of writers, according to Robertson Davies: "gushers" and "tricklers," divided by the manner in which they approach the blank page.

James Thurber was a gusher. For a story of 20,000 words he wrote a total of 240,000.

Hemingway, on the other hand, was a trickler.

"I can't write five words," Dorothy Parker once said, "but I change seven."

Gusher or trickler—each and every one of these famous authors knew the writer's secret you are about to discover. I know that because at some point in their careers, each of them was a journalist. That fact alone may not make immediate sense but stay tuned. The more you read, the more things will fall into place.

One thing is for sure: Thirty minutes from now, you are going to be equipped to write better, faster, and to greater effect than ever before.

Now don't get me wrong. I am not saying that you go in one end of this chapter a schmo and half an hour later, Shazam! Out comes a candidate for the Nobel Prize in literature. On the other hand, given the rudiments of strategy, normal intelligence, and an honest desire to make your ideas their ideas, I guarantee you will discover the rising manager within, the one who can be every bit as good on paper as in person.

But before we lay bare the so-obvious-you-don't-even-realize-they-are-there truths, do us both a favor.

Forget write-by-the-numbers rules.

Disregard the thousand and one alphabet-soup formulas for business writing.

In fact, trash every self-help program that takes intelligence and turns it into cookie-cutter thinking.

We're talking about a system so unique it doesn't just fit you, it *is* you!

A time-tested concept based on skills that are so universal they work without fail. Every time. Whether the project's a note or a novel.

Where's the fine print?

There is none.

To get us to the ins and outs of applying this surefire technique to your daily life on the job, a little background makes sense.

I've learned a thing or two minding everybody else's business. In the course of consulting with some of the country's most successful organizations I nosed into mail addressed to Pepsi-Cola managers. Analyzed annual reports of Revlon and its legion of competitors worldwide. Examined memos on environmental impact prepared by Procter & Gamble research managers. Critiqued the proposals of Mead Paper. Evaluated human relations presentations of Amerada Hess Petroleum.

What I was looking for was a secret—the difference between business writing that strikes out and business writing that strikes home.

At first, I figured the key was ideas. In the fullness of time I concluded otherwise. Too often I found myself bored by so-called important thoughts and, more frequently than you might imagine, charmed by work that was less substantial.

Grammar proved no better guarantor of success. While I do not mean to argue for anarchy, honesty compels me to say that, in my experience some of the best work intentionally broke the rules.

If it was not ideas and not syntax that marked the increment between business writing and good business writing, some X factor had to be at work. Some quality that drew substance from ideas, added form from the logic of grammar, and clarified it to produce a total greater than the sum of its parts.

Eventually, the truth revealed itself.

I had assumed all along that good business writing was due more to expression than to organization. I was off by 180 degrees. The magic turned out to reside in the underlying flow of ideas.

What crystallized things was a letter I was asked to read. Prepared by an assistant plant manager, it had gone to the head of a local parent-teacher group with a copy to the writer's boss. The boss felt the letter failed to represent the company's best interests and wondered if I agreed. I did.

> As a parent and a corporate volunteer, do I really have to tell you that we have problems in our schools? That we face those problems each and every day? That they are frustrating, and tiring, and downright debilitating? Come on now! I don't have to tell you that, do I?
>
> If I enumerated the problems in the average school in this community I would never get through.
>
> Therefore, since we don't have to talk about the problems, let's spend some time talking about solutions. There are solutions, you know. They are available. They are within your grasp, you can use them and make them work. All you have to do is go looking for them until you find them.
>
> If we paid attention to our folks, and especially our grandmothers and grandfathers we would know things weren't always like this. Back in the good old days, if a kid misbehaved at school he quickly got what for—and believe me, it was nothing compared to what was waiting for him when he got home. Pa's strap and the woodshed were a powerful combination that promised the quick application of higher learning to the seat of reason.
>
> But to tell the truth, I can't think of a city person I know who's got a woodshed today. Things have changed.
>
> That our schools have changed, too, is as evident as the reason for this letter.

The letter went on for pages but I think you get the drift. It rambled; the content wasn't entirely relevant; the folksy logic detracted from the point that time had brought changes; brevity wasn't its strong suit; and it lacked credibility.

I recall feeling grateful on reading it that my newspapering days were behind me. Otherwise, I would have been hard pressed to report the story as she presented it.

That's when I got the first glimmer that organization, the key to news reporting, is also the secret of good business writing. More specifically, a traditional form of journalistic organization handed down from editor to cub reporter since forever.

I had learned it as a third-string sports correspondent on the *Geneva Daily Times.* It is called the inverted pyramid. As the name implies, the big idea is to think of a news report as an upside-down triangle.

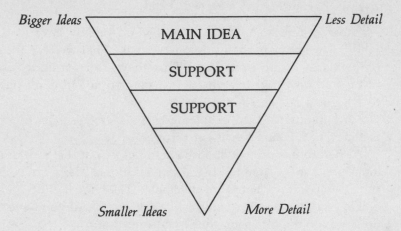

Bigger Ideas — MAIN IDEA — Less Detail

SUPPORT

SUPPORT

Smaller Ideas — More Detail

This organizes material in a way that is clear, logical, believable, and relevant. It helps the audience understand the substance of the communication instantly. That's because it transmits only what the audience needs to know in the order they need to know it.

The main idea of a news story is the same as the strategic message of a business communication. Just as the very biggest strategies have only one message, even the very longest piece of business writing is built on one *main* idea.

Because the main thought is the story's headline, it belongs at the very top of the inverted pyramid. It says what you wish the audience to do or think or believe. If they read no more than your main idea, readers should have enough information to be aware of the communication's intent.

Each level below the top supports the main idea. They are positioned in descending order of importance, moving the reader from the general to the specific, from the abstract to the concrete. The closer they come to the point of the triangle—the end of the communication—the more detail readers encounter.

My point is that the inverted pyramid informs business writing in the same way a blueprint animates construction. It forces the writer to construct sentences that articulate the *relationship* between one point and the next in a cohesive way. This lends the strong feeling of unity that enhances reader comprehension.

Now it is true that if you are writing an impassioned love letter, the best design is probably no design but love letters are rare in commerce. The first principle of effective business writing is to create the inner shape of the communication and to pursue that shape relentlessly *before* you write a word of text.

You know how it is when you sit down to write: False starts and do-overs have you tossing crumpled sheets of paper into the wastebasket as though they were basketballs. If you could just anticipate what you are getting into *before* you get into it—make changes in the flow and development of ideas when they are most easily accomplished, *before* the first draft is written—you might have more time to spend really playing hoops.

For an up-close look at the relationship between strategy and business writing, let's get down to cases.

Suppose you are the operations manager for a snack food distributor. Your boss asks for your thoughts on the location of a new satellite distribution center. Several choices are available. You think the answer is Keyville. And you are prepared to support your recommendation.

Here's the inverted pyramid that structures your story.

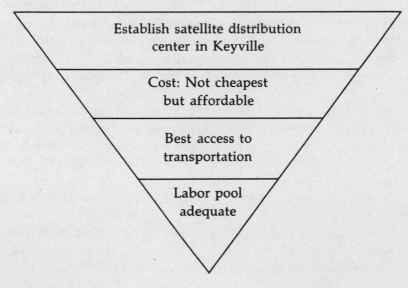

Your message, the main idea you want the target audience to act on, is built into the headline up at the very top.

Everything else—cost, access, and labor—supports the message. Think of these as convenient, bite-sized chunks the audience can swallow and digest easily.

When the communication objective of your strategy is to create awareness, the content of supporting arguments is suggested by the subject itself: functional units, relationships between events or periods, parts of a whole. For example, if you seek to make your audience aware of a new process, the supporting points might describe each phase. When the subject is the history of a product, market, or policy, milestones highlight the chain of chronology.

There are several legitimate ways to develop the impact of a concrete idea—cause and effect, and comparison and contrast are two—but what attracts people most seems to be illustration. Rather than build sentences to explain your thought, find ways to create immediacy through an illustrative image. Say you are a pharmaceutical researcher in search of a bigger R&D budget. You might liken the process of creating a new molecule to a chain reaction: Nothing happens until the budget buildup is sufficient to bring the pile to critical mass.

On the other hand, suppose your goal is to convince your target audience of a less tangible reality, that it needs to win this quarter's sales contest. Instead of the natural order imposed by the subject, you need to create a compelling rationale that encourages the audience, through a combination of logic and emotion, to accept the idea that victory is possible.

Good, we've got the shape of your communication strategically defined. Now it has the main idea and several supporting thoughts.

Next thing to decide is the unit of expression you are going to use to bring your structure to life—sentence or paragraph. The medium affects your choice. Letters and memos, most of which are one double-spaced page or less, are best driven by ideas expressed in single sentences. Longer pieces—reports, proposals, and the like—afford room to develop thoughts at greater length in paragraph form.

In either case, the building block is the simple declarative sentence.

A simple declarative sentence is just what it purports to be. It is a direct and uncomplicated combination of mostly nouns and verbs, structured to render a single thought instantly intelligible.

Framing thoughts in ways that are simple and straightforward makes your ideas not only more readable and interesting but more comprehensible to the target audience. Several landmark studies prove the point. In one, an article consisting of twenty-one sentences averaging twelve words each was found to be *seven times more comprehensible* than the same facts broken into five sentences averaging fifty-three words.

The study concludes, "Confining a sentence to a single thought is the key to comprehensibility. The basic factor is one idea, one sentence."

In the construction of simple declarative sentences do not be content with two words where one word will do, especially if the second word is an adjective or an adverb.

Following a hiccough in the pace of Dow Jones growth, my broker sent me a letter. It said, in part,

> The period of transition is being handled with considerable and effective skill, and should pass without causing undue alarm.

It is clear that "considerable" and "effective" are worse than useless. They undermine the authority of the noun they modify. "Undue," meanwhile, is simply absurd.

Eliminating the deadweight produces the following sentence:

> The period of transition is being handled with skill, and should pass.

Editing leaves the sentence 60 percent shorter. Now it comes across more active and direct—stronger! Reading between its lines reveals a more confident tonality. Since renewed confidence was the writer's objective in the first place, the edited version is more in line with his strategic needs.

If a noun or a verb cannot stand alone, propping it up with a crutch—*grateful* thanks, *true* facts, *unexpected* surprises, *undue* alarm—will not make it stronger. It will only make it redundant.

The words you employ should call up instant and readily identifiable images. Words that are definite, not vague; concrete, not abstract; and specific, not general. These arouse and build interest because they give the reader a handhold on your thinking.

Vigorous writing, the kind demanded in business, is writing in the active voice.

What's the difference between the active and passive voices?

Passive is when "Sales were increased 16.6 percent over the last quarter."

Active is when "Sales increased 16.6 percent last quarter."

Passive is when "Criteria have been established for research expenditures."

Active is when "Research expenditures meet established criteria."

Thoughts expressed in the active voice are more attractive to the ear, hence easier to grasp. They sound more energetic. Here's an added plus: Sentences written in the active voice usually require fewer words. All in all, working with active verbs quickens the pace. Your communication reads better because the energy in the words adds lift to your thoughts.

Readers are more interested in what is than in what is not. The key is the word not. It is a signal that tells the readers what follows is unimportant—don't give it a second thought. It is sometimes impossible to avoid negatives. Nevertheless, it is always a good idea to express negative things in positive ways. Instead of "not honest" make it "dishonest"; instead of "did not have confidence in" make it "distrusted."

All of which brings us to a final thought on written communication, and that is, no writer is immune from the need for rewriting. Rare is the manager who can produce perfect copy on the first try. Don't be offended if a piece of your own business writing is deficient in some respect. The crime is in not rewriting it.

So, where do we stand now on the theory and practice of business writing?

We have covered the letter and spirit of the universal elements that apply to all forms of business writing—strategic thinking, the inverted pyramid, and sentence structure. These are further developed in the sections on letters, memos, reports, and proposals.

Meanwhile, we've been distilling into several thousand words some fairly important ideas, concepts of communication that in themselves deserve small volumes.

At this point, a summing-up is in order.

The best way, I think, is to bring up the matter of Dick Guerin.

Dick, eight years out of B-school, works for Revlon. He's a rising manager in the purchasing department in charge of packaging componentry—lipstick cases, mascara tubes, eyeshadow palettes, the like. The work involves millions of dollars and has a direct and profound effect on the bottom line.

Delivery delays by a major supplier were playing havoc with production. Assembly lines were frequently down, waiting for parts that were as much as four and five working days late. This affected cash flow inasmuch as the company invoices customers on shipment. In addition, overhead increased in the form of rising inventories of unassembled parts and goods-in-process.

Working with his boss, Jim Burson, the VP for purchasing, Guerin set up a test on the number two line at Revlon's giant Edison, New Jersey, production facility. To supply it, Guerin located a qualified vendor capable of delivering parts on a just-in-time basis. The test brought several bugs to light but these were cleared up.

Now Dick was ready to make a formal recommendation to his boss.

His *target audience* was Burson, the VP for purchasing. The *communication objective* was to convince Burson to authorize a change in suppliers. His *message,* the main idea: Changing suppliers will enhance cash flow and otherwise contribute to improved margins. The *tonality* was intended to be crisp and businesslike.

Guerin's inverted pyramid, the structure of his communication, looked like this:

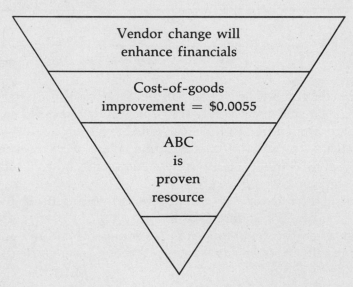

Here is the memo Dick Guerin prepared for Jim Burson:

September 20, 1991
Memorandum of Approval/Disapproval

To:　　J. Burson, VP, Purchasing

From:　R. Guerin, Purchasing Manager

Re:　　Improved Financial Results

To improve factory costs by a total of $0.0055 per unit, this recommends a just-in-time annual supply contract with ABC Molding for lipstick package componentry.

By eliminating assembly line downtime due to the present supplier's erratic pattern of deliveries, this agreement will contribute to improved cash flow equivalent to $0.003 per unit in Year 1. Further, the cost of carrying unassembled parts inventories and goods-in-process will decline on the same annual basis by $0.0025 per unit.

Our confidence in the hardness of these numbers and in the ability of ABC to perform reflects results of side-by-side tests over the last 90 days between the present supplier and ABC. ABC met or exceeded its delivery commitment on a day-in, day-out basis.

R.G.

APPROVED _____ DATE _____
NOT APPROVED _____DATE _____

Once upon a time, it was all too common for a letter or a report or a memo or a presentation to be less than it could be. The extra effort to redo it cost the most valuable resource of all—time. Now, thanks to word processing, time is less of an essence.

So, how come written business communication *still* stinks? I can think of two reasons.

First, there is the defining difference, writing itself. Everything you are up against face-to-face you are even more up against when the communication is on paper. Not only are the ever-present obstacles to getting through ever-present, the personal interactions and feedback that overcome them are unavailable.

Second and more important, written communication is in its present sorry state because human communication ability has not kept pace with technological development. It is discomforting to recognize that a lot of the rising managers I work with know more about the rigid syntax of word processing than about the more supple grammar of English.

Let's not kid each other. The system this chapter discussed cannot and does not correct for educated incapacities in an abracadabra sort of way. It takes practice since it involves careful preparation as well as writing and rewriting. Whatever the difficulties of communicating clearly on paper, however, it seems to me the risks of failing to do so are even greater.

Business is enough of a battleground without rising managers putting themselves at a competitive disadvantage by failing to use one of their best weapons: the written word.

11
LETTERS AND MEMOS

WHY LETTERS AND MEMORANDA?

Letters and memos are more than the media of business communication.

In the other guy's eyes they don't just stand for your hopes or your thoughts or your undivided interest. They *are* your hopes, your thoughts, and your undivided interest.

They are you on paper!

They articulate your point of view as only your unique self can.

Win the acceptance, action, information, materials, or special favors you need to get a leg up on the job.

Iron out problems, confirm agreements, and clear up confusion.

Promote and sell your organization and its work, products, and people.

Let others know who's where and what's what.

Create, cement, or restore relationships.

Let's put it this way: Letters and memos do for you what you would do for yourself if you could be everywhere, at once, in person!

Problems

The principal problem faced by would-be "letterati" is cost. Computer-generated form letters routinely churn out value for money. But paint-by-the-numbers approaches have their limits. There isn't a computer in the world that knows about leadership. Nor has the machine been built that can console or congratulate, admire or admonish, in quite the way a rising manager can.

Special situations demand custom communication. Without the skills to deliver the one-two punch of efficiency and effectiveness, the composition of these one-of-a-kind missives can drain more management time than the task justifies.

As if that were not bad enough, too many letters and memos that waste author time also waste that of recipients. Experts say as many as one-third of all words in business letters fail to pull their own weight and actually detract from understanding.

Opportunities

Well crafted letters and memos serve several purposes. They:
- Adequately represent the writer and his or her organization;
- Demonstrate the special importance of the recipient to the writer;
- Enable contact to be made even when the telephone proves counterproductive;
- Provide a written record that compensates for lapses of memory and helps both parties arrive at, and operate on, a common understanding;
- Offer the recipient time to consider the meaning and implications of the message;
- Encourage the discipline that focuses thinking on tight, lucid communication favoring specifics over generalities.

How to Use Model Memoranda and Letters

In the pages ahead are easy-to-use files of model memos and letters covering 35 categories of business situations. These are identified in the table of contents you will find on pages 91–93.

Once you have located the memo or letter that comes closest to meeting your particular needs, the next step is to customize it. Here strategic thinking comes into play. It will help you target your audience, select a communication objective, find a theme, and strike a tonality that will convince or convey information with clarity and assurance.

Many of the model letters and memos you will find in the pages ahead may require very little in the way of rewriting to make them appropriate for your situation. Others may benefit from additional editing. Feel free to create your own documents by combining paragraphs from two or more models.

As you create your own documents, there are several things to bear in mind.

First, because memoranda are strictly for internal consumption, think of them as letters dressed in work clothes. The ideas they communicate to others in the organization deserve as much thought, tact, and courtesy as you put into communicating with a customer, vendor, or banker. Just skip the window dressing. Because no memo should exceed one typewritten page (more than one page means you need more than one memo) there is no room for frills: Specificity and brevity are critical.

On the other hand, the first rule of letter writing is: There are no rules. A good business letter is brief, friendly, conversational, tactful, clear, and interesting.

The way memos and letters look, especially those sent outside the organization, enhances or detracts from the messages they contain. A guide to proper formatting of these vital business forms will be found on pages 164–66.

CONTENTS

10 Model Memos

25 Model Letters

Business Activities

Employees

Meetings

Orders

Quotation

Goodwill

(*Note:* The model documents that follow are presented in 35 two-page spreads. On verso pages appear strategy statements and structural outlines in inverted pyramid form. The documents articulating that strategy/structure appear recto.)

Target Audience

Andy Carson is nominally in charge of this film project. However, his boss, Ward Lance, is the key to moving the project forward.

Communication Objective

To make Ward Lance aware of an impending deadline.

Message

The selection of a production house needs to be made "yesterday."

Tonality

Crisp, businesslike, and informative.

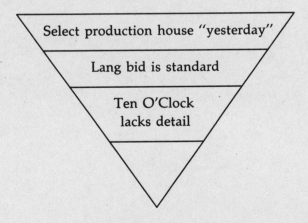

Deadline Reminder

```
Date:

To:         A. C. Carson

From:       Archer Barton

Copies to:  Messrs. F. Dedrick, W. Lance

Subject:    Deadline reminder!
```

If we are to beat what is shaping up to be a real deadline crunch, the selection of a production house needs to be made "yesterday."

Accordingly, I have reviewed production bids from Ten O'Clock Productions and from Roberts & Lang Productions.

The Lang bid follows the standard industry practice. It breaks down costs and provides sufficient detail so as to make both comparison and analysis fairly straightforward.

Because the Ten O'Clock proposal failed to break out detail, I prepared a list of items I expect the bid embraces. I've discussed these with TOP's principal and we are in agreement.

Please advise when we can discuss.

A.B.

Target Audience

John Barkman, C.F.O.

Communication Objective

To convince the target audience to approve the purchase of new software.

Message

We should buy CP Backup.

Tonality

Urgent but not emergent.

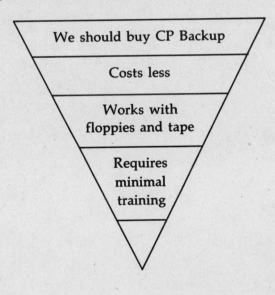

Memo: Approve/Disapprove

Date:

To: John Barkman

Copies: F. Dingell, D. Ross

From: Norman Villella

Subject: Data back up

This recommends purchase of CP Hard Disk Backup software for our PCs.

Reasons for recommendation

1. CP Backup is priced 23 to 37 percent below competition and offers features other packages can't match. These include a proprietary compression technique that stacks 60 percent more data per unit of storage.

2. Because it backs up on to floppy disks, or tape, or both, it meets the mixed requirements of our installed base.

3. Training requirements are minimal--a single 30-minute class per location.

N.V.

Approve _____ Date _____
Disapprove _____ Date _____

Target Audience

Department heads, Central Division.

Communication Objective

To create awareness of a new policy to reduce head-count within the target audience.

Message

Reducing headcount protects operating profit.

Tonality

Straightforward, businesslike.

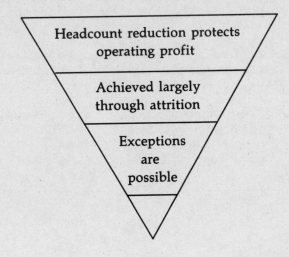

Announce Policy: Headcount Reduction

Date:

To: All Department Heads, Central Division
        H.Q.

From: Helen Nagle

Re: Policy, Headcount

To protect operating profit, division top management has determined the need for a headcount
reduction.

While this sounds very dramatic, its immediate
impact on our activities should be minimal. We
will achieve management's dollar and person tar-
gets basically through attrition. Employees who
leave the company or who elect early retirement
will not be replaced.

In the event a failure to make a staff addition
would cost us more in the long run than the
elimination of a job, I will entertain an exception to the policy.

                    H.N.

Target Audience

All employees.

Communication Objective

To convince the target audience that a smoke-free environment is a climate for success.

Message

We're gonna kick butts in 10 days!

Tonality

Compassionate yet businesslike.

We're gonna kick butts in 10 days!

Program developed in-house
by people like you for
people like you!

Announce Policy: Smoke-Free Environment

Date:

To: All Employees

From: M. Norenberg

Re: Smoke-Free Environment

Effective today, we are going to "Kick Butts in 10 Days" to become the smoke-free environment we deserve and our retail customers have long been asking for.

"Kick Butts in 10 Days" is more than a snappy slogan. It is a program we've developed in-house, based on the experiences of six of our people, hourly and managers, who have successfully broken the cigarette habit.

In the same way that fat folks know more about diets than the skinny Minnies, nobody can talk more authoritatively about putting smoking behind us than these born-again ex-smokers. I ought to know. I stopped three times before I finally quit. The attached brochure tells all.

Good luck.

                    M.N.

Target Audience

Vice President, human relations.

Communication Objective

To convince the target audience that Adam Bergen fulfills the job requirements of a new position.

Message

Adam Bergen's imagination, enthusiasm, and energy will win the kind of employee support this new position needs.

Tonality

Businesslike.

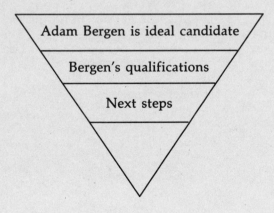

Recommendation: New Position

Date:

To: Langhorn Clay

From: Betty Laudon

Re: Recommendation to fill new position

As a result of the decision taken last week to establish a new employee ombudsman position, you asked me to recommend a candidate. After careful consideration, I have come to the conclusion that Adam Bergen, now a supervisor in the benefits group, is best qualified.

Adam has been with the organization for seven years and has risen steadily from campus recruiter to his present responsibility. His growth record is marked by imagination, enthusiasm, and energy. Each of his performance reviews has placed him in the top 10 percent on measures of skill and adaptability. He is both known and well liked throughout the division. Jean McKenzie, his assistant, is ready to fill Adam's present slot when he moves up.

Attached is the job description for Adam, which incorporates the suggestions you made when we met.

B.L.

Target Audience

All employees.

Communication Objective

To create awareness within the organization of a staff promotion.

Message

Harriet Flaum's elevation to partner is in line with our policy to promote from within.

Tonality

Warm and engaging.

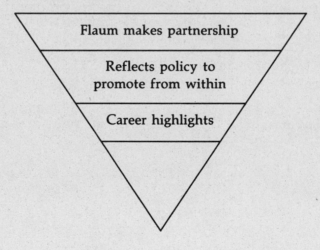

Announce Promotion

Date:

To: Staff

From: Dick Barker

Re: Harriet Flaum

Because her appointment reflects our policy to promote from within and because she so much deserves the recognition she has won, it gives me great pleasure to announce that Harriet Flaum has been made a partner of our firm.

Harriet joined Barker, Brown, Jordan six years ago to work on the Durham Group business. In the interim she has risen steadily from account representative to account supervisor to management supervisor. Prior to joining us she had been associate director of human resources for Arbold Industries, where she was responsible for executive compensation studies.

In addition to her responsibilities here at the firm, Harriet is president of the United Way Campaign in Sioux Falls and a member of the Arts Council. She is a past vice president of the League of Women Voters.

With her consistent performance and gentle manner, Harriet has won the respect of her competitors, the recognition of her colleagues, and the growing business of our clients.

I know you join me in wishing her well.

R.B.

Target Audience

Vacation policy working group.

Communication Objective

To create awareness within the target audience of the need to set objectives and develop solutions.

Message

See objective above.

Tonality

Businesslike and to the point.

Need to set objectives and develop solutions

Agenda items

Agenda, Meeting to Revise Vacation Policy

Date:

To: Dick Corbani, John Reiser, Bill Day

From: Lonny Skryzak

Re: Agenda, meeting to revise vacation policy

A meeting will be held in the main conference room between 2:00 and 3:00 PM tomorrow, March 16. The purpose of the meeting is to set objectives and develop solutions. If you wish to make additions to the agenda, please do so before the close of business today.

Subject	Purpose	Time	Presenter
Review competition	Background	5 mins.	J.R.
Staff feedback	Background	10 mins.	D.C.
Cost factors	Criteria	10 mins.	B.D.
Solutions	Brainstorm	35 mins.	All

L.S.

Target Audience

Production capacity committee.

Communication Objective

To create awareness within the target audience of the items requiring action and the persons responsible.

Tonality

Businesslike.

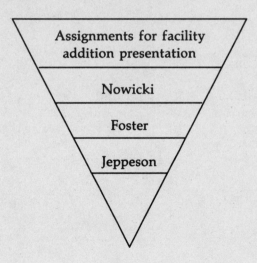

Assignments for Follow-up

Date:

To: T. Foster
        P. Jeppeson
        A. Nowicki

From: Harry Kann

Re: Assignments, presentation for new produc-
        tion facility

Action	Person Responsible	Completion Date
Develop demand by sector	A.N.	July 18
Chart: best, worst, and most likely demand	P.J.	July 16
Prepare cost estimate for 2,000 and 4,000 square-foot shop additions	T.F.	July 16

Next meeting scheduled for July 21.

                H.K.

Target Audience

Chief financial officer, Deerlot, Inc.

Communication Objective

To create awareness within the target of the Melville construction schedule.

Message

Mid-point progress report.

Tonality

Businesslike.

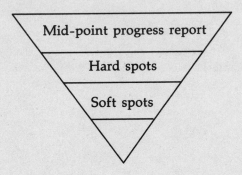

Status Report

Date:

To: Alexander Zervoulakis, Chief Financial
        Officer

From: Hal Wellington

Re: Melville construction project: progress
        report

The overall site schedule has slipped two
months, due almost entirely to the decision reported last month to change the process lines
from stainless to Pyrex.

Hard spots continue to be evident in the progress being made in new flooring and the rewiring
of the "C" building. Both of these projects are
ahead of schedule by two weeks, as a consequence
of which we will probably not need to dip into
the contingency fund.

Soft spots result from the impact of the early
freeze on the laboratory addition. No one could
have anticipated a hard freeze in early October.
The schedule, as outlined in the original proposal, was predicated on more normal tempera-
tures. Meanwhile, the main building addition was
closed in prior to the freeze and is progressing
according to plan.

                    H.W.

Target Audience

Advertising evaluation group.

Communication Objective

To create awareness within the target audience of the decision not to renew the Alpha Group contract.

Message

We have decided to review our entire promotional effort.

Tonality

Businesslike.

```
We have decided not to renew
      Alpha Group contract

    Decision prompted by
    disappointing results
```

Decision Not to Renew Advertising Contract

Date:

To: Jeanne Bill, Harvey Garrison, Enid
        Rausch, Lesley Zerega

From: Burl O'Brien

Re: Alpha Group decision

At our annual internal review yesterday, the advertising evaluation group expressed disappoint-
ment in soft sales growth for the last year. A
decision was taken not to renew our contract
with Alpha Group. By separate letter I have informed Alpha Group of this decision and asked
them to submit, ASAP, final billing.

                    B.O.

Target Audience

Former customers inactive for a year or more.

Communication Objective

To convince the target audience added benefits make renewal worthwhile.

Message

Your business is so important to us, I guarantee your satisfaction!

Tonality

Warm, friendly, concerned.

Your business so important to us,
I guarantee satisfaction

Service technician
there in an hour
or contract is free!

Prices competitive

Former Customer Follow-up

Dear Ms. Voorhees:

I wonder if you had a problem with North American Air Handlers over the last couple of years because if you did, I'd like to set things right. You see, Ms. Voorhees, I've noticed that your name has not been on our list of service contract customers for the past two years.

I'm so sure that our improved and expanded 24-hour service fleet can take care of your needs that I am willing to offer you a guarantee: Either we're at the door within an hour of your call--day or night--or we'll refund the cost of your entire service contract!

I'll telephone in a week to welcome you back to North American's satisfied customer family. Meanwhile, I'm enclosing a copy of our current service agreement so you can see for yourself the expanded capabilities we offer.

Sincerely,

Hunter Gelt
Service Manager

Target Audience

Present, satisfied customers.

Communication Objective

To create awareness within the target audience of your desire to expand.

Message

May we use your name?

Tonality

Warm, friendly, inviting.

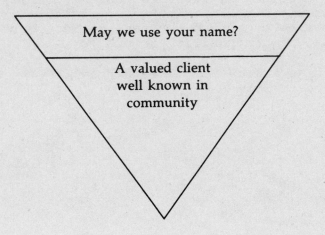

May We Use Your Name As A Reference?

Dear Mr. Gordon:

I wonder if you would be willing to allow me to
use your name when prospective clients ask for a
reference?

You have been a valued client for over ten
years, and you are well known and respected as a
merchant in our community--a perfect reference
for my small package delivery service.

I will call you in a few days for your answer.
Thank you very much.

                    Sincerely,

                    Michael Keen

Target Audience

Present customers.

Communication Objective

To create awareness within the target audience of a money-saving offer.

Message

Save 5 percent with our prepayment option.

Tonality

Friendly, businesslike.

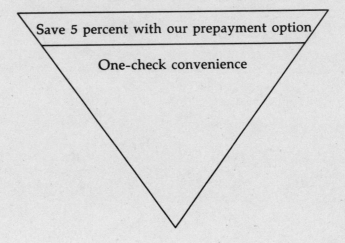

Discount Offer

Dear Mr. Rivoire:

This year we are again offering to our customers our prepayment option of a 5 percent cash discount on our seasonal mowing contract (April through November). Many of our customers prefer the seasonal mowing contract because of the convenience of writing one check and using one stamp.

If you decide to take advantage of this offer, please send us by April 30 your check for $171 for the full year's mowing. If you decide to pay monthly, the seasonal charge will total $180.

Sincerely,

Robert B. Utter

Target Audience

Present, former, and prospective customers.

Communication Objective

To create awareness within the target audience of a new business location.

Message

We are pleased to announce our new location.

Tonality

Businesslike.

We are pleased to announce our new location

Move effective March 15

Directions

New Location

Dear Mr. Shelley:

We are pleased to announce that on March 15,
Rand Management Services will be in our new location, 999 Engle Street, Englewood, New Jersey
07631. Our telephone number after the 15th will
be (201) 569-9000.

We're easy to get to. Off the Palisades Inter-
state Parkway take Exit 2, proceed one-half mile
on Palisades Avenue to the second traffic light,
and look for our new building on the near right
corner.

It is with great pleasure we extend the hospi-
tality of our new home to you on the 15th. Just
call my assistant, Binney Raines, to say how
many people will be in your party.

All of us at Rand look forward to seeing you.

                        Sincerely,

                        Michael Kresky
                        Partner

Target Audience

Current, past, and prospective customers.

Communication Objective

To create awareness within the target audience of a new profit opportunity.

Message

Here's an opportunity to double your profit.

Tonality

Upbeat yet businesslike.

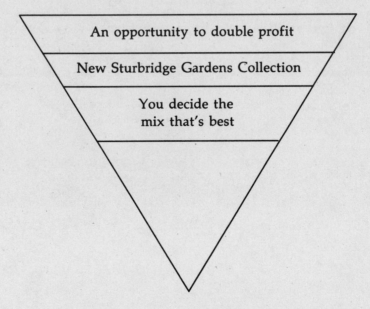

New Service or Product Line

Dear Arnie:

I have good news and I have better news. The
good news first:
 According to our records, your customers have
 made you one of the ten leading retailers of
 our Sutton line in the country.

Here's the better news.
 We have just added a new line that is likely
 to double your profit since it appeals to
 customers with a similar eye for current
 trends.

The enclosed brochure with color photographs of
each of the ten sizes in the line gives you complete measurements and prices. I'd like to ship
an introductory assortment of 100 pieces but
your sales rep, Nina Gurnsey, thinks you will be
out of stock in less than a month. What she suggests is this: Once you've had a chance to look
over the photos, we'll give you a call to put
together an introductory shipment that includes
exactly the mix that's right for your business.

 Sincerely,

 Derek van Nimwegen

Target Audience

Aggrieved customer.

Communication Objective

To convince the customer the fault was ours.

Message

It is not the computer's fault, it is mine!

Tonality

Apologetic.

Computers don't make mistakes—people do

Situation is corrected

Apology for Billing Error

Dear Mr. Govern:

As I mentioned on the phone, computers don't screw up--the people behind them do. In this case, that is me. Your check was credited to the wrong account because I failed to double-check the data entered for your account.

I am sorry for the inconvenience this may have caused but I want you to know that I have personally seen to it that we have your account information correctly entered in our data processing system.

We look forward to a continuing relationship and thank you for your understanding and your patience.

Sincerely,

Brian Sanderson

Target Audience

Dissatisfied building contractor Mal Miller.

Communication Objective

To convince the customer the shipping delay could not be foreseen.

Message

We intend to treat you as though our livelihood depends on your satisfaction . . . and it does.

Tonality

Constructive.

We intend to treat you as though our livelihood depends on your satisfaction . . . and it does

Strike was unforeseen but that doesn't solve your problem

Offer: substitute more expensive domestic goods at same price

Apology for Delay

Dear Mal:

We intend to treat you as though the very livelihood of this distributorship depends on your
satisfaction . . . and it does.

Unfortunately, the dock workers' strike in Genoa
makes it impossible to deliver the sinks you've
been so patiently awaiting. The consulate ex-
pects the strike to be over within the next
month, but I fear that may be too late for the
project you are building. Therefore, Mal, we are
prepared to substitute, at no added cost to you,
the more expensive, domestic-made sinks you
originally chose.

Let me know if this meets with your approval,
Mal. We're prepared to make delivery immediately. In the meanwhile, thanks again for your
patience.

                    Sincerely,

                    Cameron Crane

Target Audience

Mail order customer who has received the wrong product.

Communication Objective

To convince the target audience that customer satisfaction is our primary aim.

Message

Only two rules guide our business. Rule No. 1, the customer is always right; Rule No. 2, if the customer is dissatisfied, see Rule No. 1.

Tonality

Friendly.

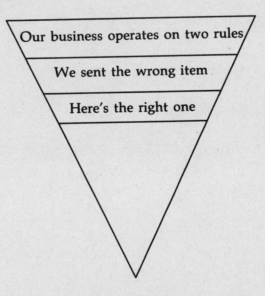

Apology for Wrong Goods

Dear Mr. Hazeltine:

Our business is built on only two rules. First, that the customer is always right. And second, when the customer is dissatisfied, refer to rule number one.

I am sorry we sent you the tray table in mahogany instead of cherry as you requested. I'm sending you the correct tray today by UPS Next Day Air. You should receive it before this letter reaches your home. I'd be grateful if you would return the one you have, using the enclosed UPS pick-up label. Just call UPS and they'll take care of everything including repacking the tray you have.

I trust this sets things right but on the off chance something is left undone, Mr. Hazeltine, please call me, toll free, at 800-855-1831. We truly appreciate your business and look forward to a long and pleasant relationship.

Sincerely,

Marjorie Cousins

Target Audience

Customer victimized by employee rudeness.

Communication Objective

To convince the audience to try our restaurant again.

Message

I can't take back what happened. But I can make sure it won't happen again.

Tonality

Warm, friendly, and apologetic.

I can't take back what happened but
I can make sure it doesn't happen again

We're a quality operation—
good food and good service

To prove the point
I'll buy you dinner

Apology for Employee Rudeness

Dear Ms. Grant:

I can't take back what happened to you at our
restaurant last night but I can assure you I
have taken steps to see that it can never happen
again. We pride ourselves on good food and good
service. With that kind of outlook, I frankly
don't see any reason for you to have been
treated as you were. So serious do we consider
the matter that the person responsible is no
longer one of our employees.

To show you how much we value your business, Ms.
Grant, I'd be grateful if you and your family
would join me for dinner, on the house, at your
convenience. Please call me and I'll be glad to
make the arrangements.

Thanks for bringing this matter to my attention.

                    Sincerely,

                    Dara Cummis

Target Audience

Professor Harold Schell.

Communication Objective

To create awareness within the target audience of the arrangements that have been made.

Message

Thank you for accepting our invitation.

Tonality

Warm and friendly.

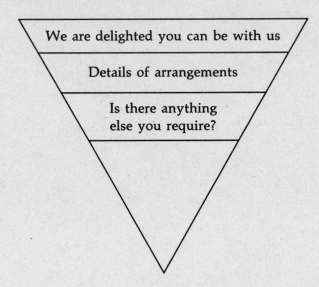

Confirming Arrangements for a Guest Speaker

Dear Professor Schell:

We are delighted you will be with us on September 18. On behalf of our president and all of the workshop participants, thank you for accepting our invitation.

I am enclosing the agenda of the luncheon program calling for you to speak for twenty minutes beginning at 12:30. Our senior vice president, Garret Burke, will introduce you. I am sure he will be in touch in a day or so to get the biographical information he needs to prepare his introduction.

Your varied experience as a consultant to many large organizations will be of particular interest to the rising managers who make up the bulk of our audience. I hope you'll devote some time to how they can prepare for further advancement into the ranks of top management.

To confirm some details, the meeting will be at the Arrowwood Conference Center, where a room has been reserved for you for the evening of September 17. If you will be kind enough to advise the hotel of your flight number, they will have a car and driver waiting when you land. Presuming your late afternoon arrival, several senior members of my staff and I would be pleased if you would join us on the evening of the 17th for an informal dinner at Chez Moi.

As agreed, Professor, we will reimburse you for all out-of-pocket expenses in connection with your appearance and, in accord with your wishes, will donate $1,500 to the American Cancer Society in the name of your nephew, Jason Kresky.

I look forward to meeting you on the 17th. In the meantime, if there is anything you require, please let me know.

Sincerely,

Harold B. Schapiro, Ph.D.

Target Audience

Job applicant submitting unsolicited resumé.

Communication Objective

To convince the target audience that a suitable job opening does not exist.

Message

It is nice to know we both agree this is a wonderful place to make a career.

Tonality

Tactful.

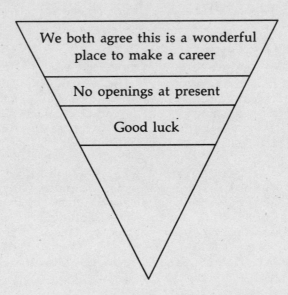

Response to Unsolicited Resumé

Dear Ms. Parker:

I guess we both agree that Hart Industries is a wonderful place to build a career. I am only sorry that we cannot offer you very much in the way of encouragement. Our policy is to fill positions for which you might qualify largely from within. To be honest, we do not foresee suitable openings for the next six months. Should this situation change, Ms. Parker, be assured I will get in touch. Meanwhile, thanks for thinking of us and good luck.

Sincerely,

Lowell Tompkins

Target Audience

Potential job candidate.

Communication Objective

To convince the target audience to accept an interview.

Message

We're looking for people like you, people with grow power.

Tonality

Enthusiastic, sell-oriented.

We're looking for people like you, people with grow power

Let's talk

Invitation to Interview

Dear Mr. Kerns:

We're looking for people like you, people with grow power. And Mike Stamp tells me you are interested in talking with us about the possibility of working as an associate with an eye toward becoming a partner.

Mike says you are a solid citizen and a substantial producer with a broad client base. Both elements fit with our track record. You see, Mr. Kerns, in the past five years we've added four partners and ten associates. And as financial planning becomes more important to our growing La Jolla community, we expect the trend to continue.

So, yes, we'd like to talk. Give me a call and we'll set up a meeting at your convenience.

Sincerely,

Van Lawrence

Target Audience

Successful job applicant.

Communication Objective

To convince the target audience to accept employment terms.

Message

Welcome aboard.

Tonality

Upbeat.

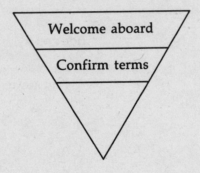

Confirm Job Offer

Dear Mr. Nichols:

This letter confirms the verbal agreement we reached over lunch yesterday. The salary is $47,500 per year. The benefits include company-paid major medical and dental coverage for you and your family. For the first five years of employment you will receive three weeks paid vacation per year plus five personal days and ten sick days. In addition, the company recognizes eleven paid holidays per year. You will be eligible for our pension plan after a one-year waiting period.

I think that about covers it, Stan. We will look forward to seeing you on Monday, April 23. Welcome aboard.

Sincerely,

Richard Potter

Target Audience

Rejected job candidate.

Communication Objective

To make the target audience aware of your decision.

Message

If you had five more years in the field . . .

Tonality

Supportive.

```
┌──────────────────────────────────────────┐
 \  If you had five more years in the field  /
  \────────────────────────────────────────/
   \      Board requires ten              /
    \     years of experience            /
     \────────────────────────────────/
      \                              /
       \                            /
        \                          /
         \                        /
          \                      /
           \                    /
            \                  /
             \                /
              \              /
               \            /
                \          /
                 \        /
                  \      /
                   \    /
                    \  /
                     \/
```

Reject Candidate

Dear Carson:

If you had five more years of experience this
letter would be very different. Your training in
social work and business administration is such
a rare combination of skills they'd be useful in
almost any senior care situation. But unfortunately, our Board of Directors is firm on their
demand for an administrator with at least ten
years of management experience in a residential
setting.

I recognize their decision is disappointing to
you and hope you see it is almost as disappointing to me. I feel you could do a terrific job
for our people and know that wherever you land,
the seniors under your care will be the better
for it.

                    Sincerely,

                    Angela Nivens

Target Audience

Prospective employer.

Communication Objective

To convince the target audience that a former employee makes a worthwhile hire.

Message

I feel like a critic reviewing a smash hit.

Tonality

Upbeat.

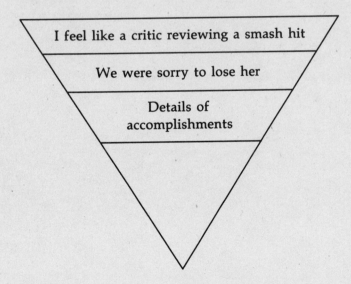

Provide a Reference

Dear Mr. Harrington:

Asking us to tell you about Harriet Feiner is like asking a critic to review a smash hit. What can we possibly add to a stunning performance?

She was with us for three years, and we were sorry indeed to learn she was moving to your part of the country. Harriet arrived at a time when our office systems were in transition from paper to computer. Everything was being handled on a catch-up basis. By the time she left, billing, accounting, personnel, and forecasting were operating in ways that were sensible and fully controlled. What is more, Mr. Harrington, she was totally responsible for hiring and training three individuals and a conversation with any of them reveals just how fair and professional she is.

If you need an office manager who is as responsible as she is skilled, you should hire Harriet Feiner.

Sincerely,

Devon Ternish

Target Audience

Executive responsible for program.

Communication Objective

To create awareness within the target audience of meeting needs.

Message

Thanks for making it all happen.

Tonality

Businesslike.

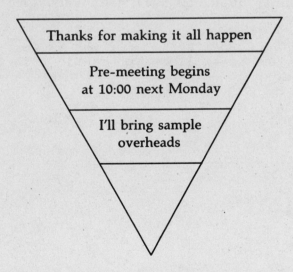

Set Up a Meeting

Dear George:

Thanks for making it happen--making the time
available next Tuesday morning, May 8, to discuss the program for mid-level managers. I'll be
at your office at 10:00 so we have a few minutes
to review formats before the group gathers at
10:30.

I'm planning to bring some overheads to give you
an idea of the materials that work with groups
like yours. I'd appreciate it if you'd arrange
an overhead in your small conference room.

I look forward to next week.

                    Sincerely,

                    Susan Woods Berkeley

Target Audience

Meeting chairperson.

Communication Objective

To make the target audience aware of a follow-up
mailing to participants.

Message

You deserve the credit . . . and here it is.

Tonality

Upbeat, warm, friendly.

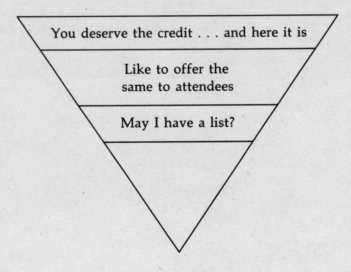

To Follow Up a Meeting

Dear Mrs. Taylor:

You deserve all the credit . . . and here it is, a coupon worth five dollars ($5) toward your next purchase of Source Cosmetics.

Thanks again for all your help in setting up my appearance and making things go so well.

I have a favor to ask, Mrs. Taylor. Is it possible for you to let me have a list of the people who attended? I'd like to thank each of them personally for their time and interest. Just jot their names and addresses on the bottom of this letter and return it to me, please.

Again, thanks for making the evening such a wonderful experience.

                    Very truly yours,

                    Inez Kurland

Target Audience

A buyer who has chosen to do business with you for the first time.

Communication Objective

To make the target audience aware of the pleasure with which this first order has been received.

Message

This is more than an opening order. It's the beginning of a relationship.

Tonality

Gracious.

This is more than an opening order. It's the beginning of a new relationship

Order ships this week

Our representative will call

Acknowledge First Order

Dear Mr. Joachim:

Your purchase order for 6,000 HubCraft TrailMaster Bushings--which ship on Tuesday via Yellow Freight--represents more than an opening order. It is the beginning of what we expect will be a long and mutually profitable relationship between our companies.

I've asked Richard Conning, our chief sales engineer, to call on you soon to recommend the best HubCraft products for all your needs, routine and special. You'll be hearing from him in the next few days. Meanwhile, thank you for your confidence in HubCraft.

Sincerely,

Carl Binns

Target Audience

Irate customer.

Communication Objective

To create awareness of an honest error.

Message

There's sometimes an unexpected price to be paid for success.

Tonality

Tactful, constructive.

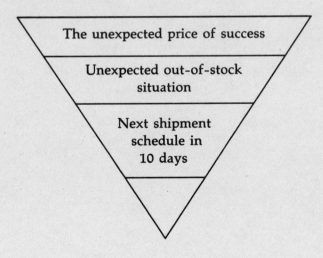

Late Delivery

Dear Mrs. Sommers:

When Leila Zahn took your order for sixteen
pieces of our popular Fatto A Mano toddlers
jacket, the one featured in the Children's Wear
section of the <u>New York Times</u>, she was sure we
could make immediate delivery to meet your September 14th promotion date. I would have made
the same promise, Mrs. Sommers, because our running inventory of this jacket is several months'
supply.

Neither of us was prepared to learn that our entire stock had been cleaned out by Dingman's in
Santa Cruz. Of course, we immediately telephoned
Italy to order a large resupply and have been
promised delivery by the 16th. The question is
this: May we hold your order until then? To
speed things up we'll have your sixteen pieces
shipped Air Express directly from Milan. You
should receive them by the 16th, possibly a day
or two earlier.

I am delighted to see you doing such a wonderful
job with the jacket. Leila joins me in wishing
you a smashing fall season.

                    Sincerely,

                    Angela Corbin

Target Audience

Buying authority.

Communication Objective

To create awareness within the target audience of vendor's capabilities.

Message

May we have the opportunity to quote?

Tonality

Formal, businesslike.

May we have the opportunity to quote?

Our background and experience

Suggest meeting
next Thursday

Request to Quote

Dear Mr. Hamilton:

This requests an opportunity to quote for this
year's snow removal contract.

SnoGone has been in the snow removal business
for twenty-two years, serving municipal and
large industrial and institutional clients.
These include the City of Wallingford, Bliven
Electronics, The Harwell School, and Mercy Medi-
cal Center. We are known among these and dozens
of others as a responsive and responsible company providing prompt service on a cost-
effective basis.

I should like to meet with you to discuss your
snow removal needs so that we may submit a
quote. May I see you next Friday morning? I will
call on Monday to see if this is convenient.

Sincerely,

Kenneth P. Rambling

Target Audience

Prospective customer.

Communication Objective

To convince the prospect to approve proposal.

Message

Several conditions require treatment.

Tonality

Businesslike and formal.

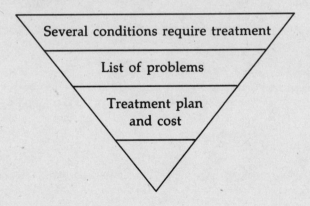

Proposal

Dear Mr. Calhern:

During my March 3 inspection of your property we found black vine weevils infesting the rhododendrons that surround your house. They are a serious problem and need to be controlled as soon as possible. In addition, there is powdery mildew affecting the shrub garden along the front borders, and the evergreens have tip blight.

We recommend five treatments per year for the shrubs and trees. These include dormant oil in late winter to destroy insect eggs, followed by treatments in early spring, late spring, and summer for continuing suppression. In the late fall, we will apply sufficient fertilizer to encourage healthy root growth and to keep plants strong through the winter. The chemicals we use are harmless to humans, pets, and livestock, and are applied by state-certified horticulturists.

Each treatment costs fifty-one dollars ($51). There is a 10 percent discount for payment in full, in advance. If you are not pleased with the results of any treatment we will retreat your trees and shrubs at no additional cost. You may discontinue service any time you wish.

As you can see, Mr. Calhern, we have set up the program so you have nothing to lose and a better landscape to gain. I will telephone on Monday to arrange the schedule of treatments.

Sincerely,

Luther Potts

Target Audience

Newly promoted executive.

Communication Objective

To create awareness within the target audience of the sender's continuing business interest.

Message

Nobody here was surprised!

Tonality

Warm, engaging, friendly.

It came as no surprise to us

Congratulations on
your promotion

Congratulations on Promotion

Dear Millicent:

It came as no surprise to us that Farnsworth International recognized real talent when it saw
same. They've got a terrific reputation for se-
lecting the best.

Give 'em hell, woman!

                    Regards,

                    Miriam Headly

Target Audience

A longtime customer and friend.

Communication Objective

To create awareness within the target audience of a supplier's heartfelt congratulations.

Message

We're delighted for two reasons.

Tonality

Friendly.

Delighted with your article for two reasons

First, it really says something

Second, because you are a
longtime friend
and customer

Congratulations on Article

Dear Melvin:

I was delighted with your article in <u>Plant Engineering</u> for two reasons. First, because it calls for the dynamic leadership our profession requires in these moments of transition. And second, because the honor of authorship was bestowed on a longtime friend and customer.

                    Sincerely,

                    Frank Don Tompkins

Target Audience

Satisfied customer.

Communication Objective

To make the target audience aware of appreciation for their patronage.

Message

What pleases you pleases us.

Tonality

Personal and friendly.

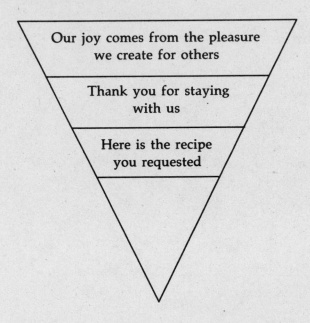

Acknowledge a Compliment

Dear Mr. and Mrs. deWinter:

Our joy in running Old Rover Inn comes in knowing that by working to do our best, we create
the pleasurable experiences our guests come here
to find. It is a pleasure made all the greater
when friends of the Inn are as gracious as you
and take the time to share their experience.

Our chef, Jim Gaines, was delighted to know you
enjoyed the salmon mousse and was pleased to
prepare the enclosed recipe.

On behalf of Jim, my wife Rita, and the entire
staff here at the Old Rover Inn, thank you. We
look forward to seeing you again in the near future.

Sincerely,

G. Vernon Gates

Target Audience

The family of a deceased colleague.

Communication Objective

To make target audience aware the loss is felt beyond the family.

Message

It is a sad thing to write a letter like this.

Tonality

Consoling.

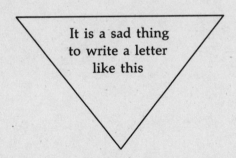

Sympathy

Dear Marie:

It is always a sad thing to write a letter like this but particularly so in this case. Everyone at the office was very sorry to learn of Marco's untimely death. He was such a smiling presence in our lives. People said it was a pleasure to do business with a place in which the customer came first--and that was certainly Marco's philosophy. We will miss him.

Our sympathy,

Rinaldo diBlasi

Format: Memoranda

Letterhead

triple space
Date:
double space
To:
double space
Copies to:
double space
From:
double space
Subject:
triple space

First paragraph (begins flush left and single spaced).
double space
Succeeding paragraphs
double space between each
Last paragraph
double space
Writer's initials, centered

Format: Letters

Letterhead

1 to 12 blank lines depending on length of letter (for shorter letters leave more blank lines)

Date

1 to 12 blank lines depending on length of letter (for shorter letters leave more blank lines)

Person's name
Title
Company name
Street address
City, State, Zip
    double space
Dear (salutation):
    double space
First paragraph, body of the letter begins.
(This is always single spaced with the
paragraphs starting at the left margin or
indented five spaces.)
    double space
Next paragraph
    double space
Sincerely yours,
    quadruple space

Typed name
Title
    The format for the second page of a two-page letter is shown on page 166.

6 blank lines from top of page

Name of person who is receiving letter
Page 2
Date
triple space

All paragraphs begin at the left or indented
five spaces.
double space
Last paragraph
double space
Sincerely yours,
quadruple space

Typed name
Title

12

REPORTS AND PROPOSALS

WHY REPORTS AND PROPOSALS?

In the process of creating more informed audiences, reports and proposals monitor progress, observe events, collect information, evaluate conditions, analyze situations, provide a historical record, and formulate plans for future action.

They come in a bewildering variety of forms, everything from the one-page quickie explaining why there is trouble in the customer services department to the formal documents publicly held companies are required to file with the Securities and Exchange Commission.

What characterizes them is what distinguishes them from the letters, memos, and manuscripts they sometimes resemble: objective accuracy.

Their overriding goal is to provide information in ways that are clear and accessible. This they achieve when they eschew personal bias and opinion to provide sound conclusions drawn from information that is accurate, concrete, and comprehensive.

Because almost any written communication can be considered a report, a precise definition is hard to come by. So let's finesse a formal characterization by saying that what we are really talking about is a broad array of management tools—written, factual accounts that shed light on the business, its organization, and the degree to which it fulfills its charter.

Seen through the lens of strategic thinking, reports invariably examine the consequences of past decisions. By opening windows on what has been and is, they feed back the perspective from which effective management analyzes events, monitors and adjusts performance, evaluates results, and sets forth accountability.

Proposals, on the other hand, are reports dressed up in selling clothes. They play more to the forward-looking vision of decision makers by offering views onto the business landscapes of tomorrow. To paraphrase novelist Joseph Conrad, every proposal is a report secretly intended to convince its readers that it represents the authentic history of an age to come.

Problems

Although in three out of four respects developing the strategy of a report is a straightforward matter, many rising managers face something of an identity crisis when it comes to the communication objective.

To set the record straight:

Because they are intended to furnish information and so deal in matters of past and contemporary events, *reports are always targeted to create awareness,* though, as a by-product, they may also develop conviction.

Proposals, on the other hand, *are always positioned to create conviction—to convince the target audience to travel a new and possibly different road.*

Opportunities

Reports and proposals are often the only form of contact between a rising manager and the organization's movers and shakers. Really good documents—the ones that quietly draw favorable attention to their authors and so begin to make their reputations—share several elements.

Accuracy: Good reports tell the truth and nothing but the truth. In ways that are relevant, specific, and concrete, they are long on data, nouns, and verbs, and short on opinions and adjectives.

Perspective: Lies are never pretty, even when they come about because you decide to omit details that undermine your position. For example, to report that sales rose last quarter by 24 percent without mentioning that the rise was due entirely to one order misleads readers to inappropriate actions and poor decisions.

Draw conclusions only from the assembled data: Even if you have strong feelings about the subject, do not allow personal gripes and biases to enter your findings.

Thou shalt not copy. Unless instructed otherwise, when you write a report at the request of your boss, *only* your boss is entitled to see it.

Structure

Certain highly specialized documents may need to hew to rigid regulatory-agency or academic formats, but most do not. No matter what form it takes—and any form that suits is acceptable—every report's universal mission is to be more valuable than the raw data it represents.

Model Proposal

Date

To: Mr. Arthur Tracey, Vice President, Operations

From: Nicholas Rivas

Dear Mr. Tracey:

This memo is a proposal to develop a company newsletter for ABC East. This newsletter's purpose is:
  1. To acquaint employees with quality of the work experience at ABC, thereby to show the company as a good place in which to build a long-term career.
  2. To create a family feeling among employees.
  3. To develop a vehicle through which top management can provide authoritative information about plans and policies.

Background

ABC East has grown rapidly over the last several years, making the task of keeping employees informed increasingly difficult.

When the company was small, frequent company-wide meetings, bulletins, and social functions served to keep everyone up-to-date.

Now, with nearly a thousand people, lines of communication have grown increasingly long. Not only is it more difficult to keep employees informed these days, ABC has also lost the continual flow of feedback from employees that enabled management to keep a finger on the pulse of the organization.

Plan

  A. Frequency/format: This recommends a monthly publication of a tabloid size (11 1/2" × 15") newspaper consisting of eight pages.
  B. Content: Although reports of company oper-

ations should be covered, at least 75 percent of space available will be devoted to promotions, personal items (births, marriages, deaths), recreational activities, letters to the editor, and employee photographs.

C. <u>Design</u>: Masthead, typography, layouts, and graphics specifications will be developed by Editorial Consultants, Inc., of Detroit, an editorial development consultancy to four of the first ten companies on the Fortune 500 list.

D. <u>Writing</u>: A publication that reads like a management memo will fail to achieve the goals established for this project. To ensure that the language is personal, simple, and conversational, a style handbook will be prepared by a committee composed of several nationally recognized professors of journalism and headed by Dr. George Bunting, Dean of the Graduate School of Journalism at the state university.

E. <u>Staff</u>: This proposes a three-person staff consisting of an editor-in-chief, a reporter/photographer, and a production editor.

F. <u>Cost</u>: Including charges for direct hires, overhead, production, and distribution, per-copy costs will be $1.27 in Year I, $1.31 in Year II, and $1.33 in Year III.

Recommendation

1. Approve this proposal for an employee newspaper to be issued under the supervision of the Vice President for Human Relations.

2. Approve the employment of an editor-in-chief and two staff members.

3. Appoint a publication advisory group consisting of one representative from each major department to assist the editor in determining overall editorial direction.

Model Report

MANAGEMENT REPORT

Operating Results

June

Revenue   Operations produced revenues of
                 $9.85MM, an increase of 11% vs.
                 year ago, and + $.769MM vs. bud-
                 get.

Income   Net operating income, at
                 $1.26MM, was ahead of budget
                 $182M and exceeded the prior
                 year by 6.3%.

Cost   Monthly expenses were favorable
Containment   to plan by 1.5% due principally
                 to a reduction in energy costs.

Year to Date

Revenue   Operating revenues for the
                 first six months were 12% ahead
                 of last year, net of inflation.

Income   Net operating profit declined
                 1.2% as a result of one-time
                 charges.

Ameroplan Division

Revenue

Operations produced revenues of $6.21MM, an increase of 14% vs. year ago, and + $.520MM vs. budget. In line with historical trends, department stores, 15% of accounts, generated 83% of revenues. The increasing (though still minor) importance of chain drug stores was offset by a decline in mass volume retailers.

Income

Net operating income of $0.32/ case was ahead of budget 4% and exceeded the prior year by 2.1%.

Cost Containment

More stringent asset management reduced receivables, as expressed in days sales outstanding, by 1.1 days; and costs associated with inventories declined $421M.

Eurotherm Division

Revenue

Operations produced revenues of $3.65MM, an increase of 10.4% vs. year ago, and + $.181M vs. budget. Increases are due primarily to growing consumer acceptance of more sophisticated skin treatment systems.

Income

Net operating income of $0.0832/case was 1% below budget but exceeded the prior year by 5.91%.

Cost Containment

Manufacturing costs are high in relation to the budget. This is due entirely to temporary inefficiencies resulting from unan-

ticipated market demand. As in-
ventory-to-sales ratios improve
over the next two bi-weekly periods, costs will return to trend-
line.

Year Ahead
Hard Spots vs. Soft Spots

Hard spots   Initial bookings for the holiday
season are running at a rate 12%
favorable to budget and generally
in line with forecasts. In new
product development, Eurotherm
Division will introduce 74 new
SKUs for shipment beginning in
September. Meanwhile, Amero-
plan's major shade promotion,
Hopscotch, continues to attract
record bookings as it proceeds on
target for release September 1.

Soft spots   Headquarters head count remains
thirty-six heads or $1.44MM over
budget and appears refractory to a
policy of attrition. Provision
for uncollectible accounts will
impact in the third quarter and may
reduce income by as much as $0.02
per share.

13

SPEECHES AND PRESENTATIONS

WHY SPEECHES AND PRESENTATIONS?

"To sum up: unstoppable social and economic trends will continue to drive demand for low-calorie lifestyles. That's why the diet category is going to remain the single best-selling product group in the entire store." Thus concludes a chain-store executive speaking before a workshop of regional supermarket operators.

Meanwhile, several time zones to the west, a 34-year-old entrepreneur quietly supplements the thrust of her argument with a series of visual aids. She tells men and women seated at the table, who represent a consortium of lending institutions, that reorganizing the way her Silicon Valley company supports its software products will not only lead to more satisfied customers, it will lead to more customers, period!

At about the same time, a group of managers gathers in Tampa. There the speaker, a rising human resources executive, tells of a policy initiative that is entirely new and wholly unprecedented. This remarkable innovation will enable the company's total work force—hourly and salaried—to participate in stock-option plans formerly reserved exclusively for management.

And later that night, at a retirement dinner, a drug company research chemist will bid farewell to his mentor, Doctor Eleanor van Beardsley. In his after-dinner remarks he says she has been an effective voice in Washington for more enlightened patent policies and the company will sorely miss her.

Whether they persuade bankers to go for a deal, motivate employees to go the extra mile, or simply better inform the conduct of affairs in ways that are compelling, clarifying, and articulate, the common thread in these examples is the use of human speech to carry a business message.

Thanks largely to complementary trends toward employee empowerment on the one hand and corporate decentralization on the other, a manager's ability to speak effectively has taken on fresh importance in recent years. Working closer to their own people and to their markets, managers are finding it increasingly necessary to leverage their time by personally informing, inspiring, and persuading groups within and beyond their organizations.

Given a working environment that more and more emphasizes verbal salesmanship, business speeches and presentations (which are speeches supported by visual aids) are emerging as possibly the most effective media—and certainly the ones offering the greatest immediacy—available to managers seeking to get ahead in the organization.

Problems

The good news:

Nothing raises a manager's stock faster, or gives greater visibility, than a well rendered speech or presentation.

The not-so-good news:

Nothing raises a manager's anxiety higher than the prospect of having to make one.

Several reasons conspire to cloak the public speaking process in an air of jeopardy.

For one thing, speeches are seen as more personal than written forms of business communication. Audiences tend to identify managers with the messages they deliver (which explains why, when you are called on to deliver a slab of bad news, it is a good idea to sandwich it between a couple of slices of happier tidings).

A second and closely related problem emerges out of the seemingly casual attitude some rising managers have toward speaking situations. Unlike the importance they attach to the written word, which they know has a life beyond its initial purpose, they see public speaking as more ephemeral, an extension of conversation here one minute and gone the next. These shoot-from-the-lip speakers fail to recognize what can prove painful: You can never cross out what you just said. It often turns out that the dumbest thing you articulate ends up the most memorable.

Consistent success is no accident. As with any serious business communication, speaking impressions need to be managed. Good results emerge when you tailor what you are going to say and how you are going to say it to suit the audience and its state of mind.

Unlike written documents, spoken communications do not afford the audience the opportunity to read, reread, and thoughtfully consider at leisure each of the arguments being made. Quite the contrary. Each point must be rendered in a way that instantly relates to the thought that has preceded it while preparing the audience to accept as both logical and inevitable the ideas that are yet to be voiced.

The Opportunity

With only modest adjustments in thinking to compensate for the factors affecting audience recall and timing, the strategic process that makes your ideas their ideas through letters, memos, reports, and proposals works as well in developing speeches for sales meetings, award ceremonies, civic functions, and business conferences.

As you have seen in earlier chapters, the approach is based not on rigid and often irrelevant formulas but on a handful of fundamental skills that, once learned, work all the time. Employing everyday common sense, normal business judgment, and intelligent flexibility to target the audience, identify your communication objective, and develop a theme and tonality, the system obliges you to make choices about what to say and how to say it in ways that are faithful to your goals and the needs of your listeners.

The constellation of differences that set oral apart from written communications orbits around the closely related issues of audience recall and timing, particularly as these affect the structure of the talk.

Several factors work against the ability of an audience to absorb a speaker's message.

Foremost among these is the undisputed scientific finding that audience recall *is inversely proportional to the amount of information presented.*

In one published experiment, a business speaker made a fifteen-minute talk using a total of fourteen points. After only twenty-four hours, most of the audience was unable to recall the substance of the remarks. About 30 percent remembered two points but fewer than two out of a hundred were able to dredge up four or more points.

In other words, had the speaker simply covered fewer topics—two points instead of fourteen—he would have been not twice or seven times better. *He would have been at least fifteen times more effective.* The conclusion: when it comes to speeches and presentations, *ideas are always more important than details!*

Audience recall is further affected by the failure of many speakers to recognize that *the end of a speech or presentation produces the impression the audience takes home.* To hit home, the close needs to be a memorable and compelling statement of the talk's main idea.

Third is the effect of vocabulary on receptivity. It is hard enough to sustain a train of thought under normal circumstances. When your vocabulary is unfamiliar (or when you try to prove how smart you are) the difficulty is increased, often to the point where listeners who have to stop to think about the meaning of each unusual word miss your point and muddle along without knowing what was said. Readers can take their time but listeners need to understand each word in the time it takes to enunciate it—*an average of half a second!*

Put plain, the way to talk *to* people is to talk *like* the people you wish to reach. Stick to words that they normally use. The whole idea is to make them feel that what you have to say is what is on their minds.

Structure

Having examined the factors that affect the ability of an audience to understand what you are saying, the next question would-be speakers need to consider is structure.

With the exception of the ending, the outline of a speech should resemble the inverted pyramid of other strategic business documents. This, you will recall, organizes your material in a way that is clear, logical, relevant, and believable. It helps the audience understand the substance of your speech by positioning what they need to know in the order in which they need to know it.

It begins with the single most important idea—the one contained in your message. This says what you wish the audience to do or think or believe. It is followed *immediately* by a supporting point that reinforces the credibility of the main thought.

If the message is that the data-processing department needs to be reorganized, the support for that point—the reason the audience should believe it—lies in the fact that a reorganized D-P function will produce more timely and actionable reports at lower unit cost.

Each succeeding level in the pyramid may be an independent idea of lesser importance than the first, or a subordinate thought that contributes to or amplifies the idea immediately above it.

Because the chain of idea-support-idea-support positions the points you wish to make in *descending* order of importance, listeners are transported from the general to the specific, from the abstract to the concrete.

It is only at the end that a speech departs from the strategic template of other documents.

As in any sound sales proposition, the close of a speech asks for the order. But instead of seeking a signature on the dotted line, it asks for audience acceptance. This is accomplished by reprising the main idea—concluding by telling the audience, in a fresh and memorable way, what it is you wish them to do or think or believe:

"To conclude, our studies have shown that we need to do three things to improve our data-processing performance: simplify the infrastructure, install state-of-the-art equipment, and revamp reporting relationships. Making these improvements may not result in more decisions. But one thing's for sure: it will certainly yield better ones."

Timing

Part of the art of speech making lies in filling allotted time without exceeding the limits imposed by schedules. Remember, when you speak before twenty-five people and go just sixty seconds over your allotment, you do not spend a mere extra minute: You squander twenty-five extra minutes, none of which belongs to you in the first place.

In ordinary conversation, thoughts are exchanged at the rate of roughly 125 to 150 words per minute. A somewhat slower rate is preferable for public speaking, in the neighborhood of 100 words per minute. This translates to about two minutes per standard typewritten page.

Presuming your speech seeks to make three basic points and the time allotted is ten minutes, you could safely explain each of these thoughts in about two minutes, using roughly one page per point; devote an additional two minutes to thank your host and otherwise open the talk; and a final two minutes to wrap it up.

On the other hand, if you have been given thirty minutes for the same talk, you could spend a total of twenty-four minutes developing your major ideas and still have three minutes at the top and bottom of your remarks to establish rapport, provide an overview, and develop the closure you seek.

Given a choice of making the talk in ten minutes or using up thirty is more temptation than most novice speakers can resist. Try to remember that in speaking, as in architecture, the wisdom of Mies van der Rohe prevails—"Less is more." It is never a good idea to rush a speech, but you pad one out at your own peril.

CBS newscaster Charles Osgood, instructing listeners on how to make a speech, reminded them that the standard length of a vaudeville act was twelve minutes: "If all those troupers singing and dancing their hearts out couldn't go on for more than twelve minutes without boring the customers, what makes you think you can?"

Experienced public speakers take no more time than is necessary to get their ideas across.

Visual Aids

It is not by accident that in most, if not all, network television commercials—the ones on which advertisers lavish the greatest amounts of effort, talent, research, and vulgar amounts of money—a line of type reprising the main message flashes across the screen as the voice of an on- or off-camera narrator intones word-for-word the selfsame message.

This practice reflects the well-documented communication

Outline for a Ten-minute Talk with Notes on Timing and Space

Subject	Time	Pages
I. Salutary remarks	2	1
II. We still treat women like second-class citizens.		
A. If we continue to make artificial distinctions between goals of women and goals of business, everyone is short-changed.	3	1½
III. This is self-defeating because when it comes to sound business leadership and responsible entrepreneurship, sex doesn't count.		
A. Estée Lauder		
B. Mary Wells Lawrence		
C. Katharine Graham	4	2
IV. These exceptional women dramatize the point: in business, women are a uniquely underdeveloped asset.		
A. Vis-à-vis the number of female managers there are few female CEOs.	1	½
V. The wheels of progress grind slowly but grind they do. Things are more promising than ever.		
A. Women are moving up.		
B. The failed ERA changed attitudes.		
C. Everything needn't change for things to be different.		
D. Competition will produce more improvement because no business can afford to neglect one of its two most precious corporate resources.	2	1
Total	12	6

research finding: the memorability of an idea is dramatically and invariably improved by its graphic superimposition.

What is true of network audiences is just as true of business audiences: Properly used, visual aids actually increase one's ability to absorb what is being said.

This is not to argue that graphics and other visual aids have a place in every speech. When the message is highly emotional, for example, visual aids may prove more of a mood breaker than an enhancement. On the other hand, when a presentation is complex—particularly where numbers and trends are involved—visuals can help the audience more easily track the flow of your thoughts.

Whatever form visuals take—flip charts, overheads, slides—several universal guidelines apply.

- Think of each graphic as a highway billboard. Eliminate everything that doesn't contribute to a clear understanding of the point at fifty-five miles per hour.
- One idea per visual.
- Illustrate only the major points, not the details.
- Wording, in large, clear, upper-and-lower-case type, should be terse (Not More Decisions. Better Decisions!)
- Telegraph the meaning of charts (line, pie, bar) with a simple explanatory headline (Demand Price Elastic).
- Never paraphrase. Without fail, read the text of every headline, word-for-word, exactly as it appears in the visual aid.

CONTENTS

A Portfolio of Speeches

(*Note:* The model documents section, which follows, is written in six two-page layouts. Each of these begins on a verso page with a strategy statement. The document representing that strategy begins recto.)

To Introduce a Speaker

Target Audience

All those attending the annual meeting.

Communication Objective

To create awareness within the target audience of the keynoter's credentials.

Message

At his company, where the track is fast, the numbers are big, and the competition is fierce, Duane Berlin is a stand-out.

Tonality

Upbeat, enthusiastic, warm.

Several years ago, Michael Jackson said a mouthful.

"If we want to change the world," Michael sang, "we start by looking in the mirror."

That is, of course, what this evening is all about--looking into the mirror of business reality to see just how, and how much, this organization has changed the face of opportunity in our corner of America.

Our keynote speaker's company took Michael Jackson's words to heart.

It stands today as living proof that in this country, a corporate giant can never be anything more than the people of that organization want it to be.

I am happy to say that the women and men of this fine organization have told us and shown us just how much they want to be our partners in progress.

One of those people is our speaker this evening.

At his company, where the track is fast, the numbers are big, and the competition is fierce, Duane Berlin is a stand-out.

Now contrary to the opinion of obstetricians, nothing happens overnight . . . not even to Duane.

After all, it took him almost thirty-six months to move to the top.

He joined the company as senior vice president of marketing.

Two years later they made him executive vice president of marketing and national sales.

And just this September he moved into the corner office, the one reserved for the head honcho.

He's the man behind the company's marketing strategy, the program that's tied major entertainment and sports properties to its national advertising campaigns.

In addition, Duane's seventeen-year background in marketing includes top positions at Apple Computer, International Playtex, and Bristol-Myers.

If efficiency is doing the thing right . . . and effectiveness is doing the right thing, here is a past master at both.

Ladies and gentlemen, it is an honor to present your keynote speaker, a fellow who more than lives up to his goals, a man who lives up to his potential, Duane Berlin.

Inspirational Meeting Opener

Target Audience

All those in the audience.

Communication Objective

To convince the target audience that the annual meeting is intended to be a creative learning experience.

Message

We have come together to embark on a voyage of discovery.

Tonality

Upbeat.

Good morning.

We have come together to embark on a voyage of discovery.

For a brief moment, I hope you will join me.

Bring your minds back to the first time you ever discovered something on your very own. Maybe something as simple as discovering that a bathtub toy floats on water.

Perhaps it was later when you were struggling with the multiplication table and the magic moment came when you discovered the reason behind it.

Whatever the occasion, try to remember what it was you felt in that moment of awakening.

Joy.

Exhilaration.

Surely your mind rejoiced in that instant of fresh awareness.

It was the joy of learning that made your life not only brighter but forever different and better.

This morning we find ourselves again on the edge of a new tomorrow.

Through the ideas and insights that will be offered in the meetings that we begin now, to all of us will come the chance to discover again the satisfaction of becoming more than we have ever before been.

It is an opportunity to be cherished, for in exploring our business we will discover more than answers.

We will discover opportunity itself.

It is with great pleasure I welcome you to our annual meeting.

A Sales Training Talk

Target Audience

Training managers.

Communication Objective

To convince the target audience to end speeches on a strong note.

Message

The only way to keep from owing the audience money is to plan the end of the meeting first.

Tonality

Warm, supportive, happy, authoritative.

Mark Twain tells a story about a preacher and
his sermon.

When the speaker had been going for five minutes, Twain was willing to drop two dollars in
the collection plate.

When the preacher had passed the ten-minute
mark, he was willing to put out a dollar.

But when the sermon had been going for thirty
minutes, Mark Twain said, "Hell, the man owes *me*
twenty!"

Five minutes, two dollars; ten minutes, one
dollar; thirty minutes, not a red cent. That's
the way it is with sales training meetings.

One way to keep from owing the audience money
is to plan the end of the meeting first.

That may sound like putting the cart before
the horse but believe me, when your business,
like mine and the preacher's, deals in ideas, it
makes a lot of sense.

You see, the finish is the part the audience
takes home. In fact, some speakers write the end
of their speech first and then go back to create
the start and the middle parts.

The same idea is true for sales meetings.

It is a simple strategy based on the revolu-
tionary idea of last things first.

When you sit down to write, ask yourself this
question: What do I want them to do and how will
they do it?

The answers to those two questions will give
you a clear picture of what you want to close
on.

If you are selling an idea, it is always wise
to mention it up front. But it is a mistake not
to bring it up again at the end. In fact,
there's plenty of research to show that folks
are most likely to remember it if you bring it
in again at the end.

Probably one of the most dreaded moments in
any businessperson's life is being put on the
spot at a business meeting to say a few words on
this or that.

Slowly you get to your feet.

Even more slowly you hem and haw.

And to no one's regret you finally and lamely
end on something like this: "Well, that's all
I've got to say."

Too many meetings end the same way--with a whimper instead of a wallop!

Now I am going to give you a tip that will make you seem like Einstein next time your boss puts you on the spot to say a few words.

Listen carefully because what I am about to tell you may strike you as strange.

Don't--I say don't--think for even a second about what you are going to say to open your remarks.

Instead, my friends, devote all the time you've got to how you are going to close.

That's right--I am telling you not to worry about what you'll say at any time except in that minute before you sit down.

And what you should think about is one, two, three.

You heard me right. Think about one, two, three--because that is what you are going to say.

What you must remember, you tell the folks, is one (then make your first point); two (make your second point); and three (make your last point).

Now sit down and you will find you have made a memorable impression.

So when the boss says he is going to call on you for a few remarks, don't try to figure out what you are going to say to start things off. If you try to work out a complete speech you'll never get it done. But you almost always have time for the three-step finish.

Get that end worked out.

Then, when it is time to rise, get up slowly, start on a low beat, say what comes to mind on the topic and then throw your bang-up finish at them.

First, go jump in the lake.

Second, swim out.

Third, hang yourself out to dry.

When you sit down, your organized ending will make them think you are one smart dude.

Does it work?

Well, just last week I got a letter from a fellow I had told about the old one-two-three. He said, "Mister, that's a swell suggestion. I tried it out last week. Didn't have a thought in my head but I took your tip and wowed them. So

much so the boss assigned me to carry out the
project. I've been working overtime ever since.
If you have any more suggestions like that--
well, I think you know where you can put them."

That's gratitude for you.

But it proves my point. It's as easy as one-
two-three.

I am spending this much time on the ending,
my friends, because the finish is the weakest
part of most speeches and presentations.

It doesn't have to be that way.

Work with your people who are called upon to
speak and teach them to go out with a bang.

You'll be surprised at what happens.

People who can't speak actually get their
ideas across.

The ones who fumble and fumfer do things more
easily.

The ones who give the impression of being un-
certain come across as experts.

Believe me, teaching your people this little
secret will pay off for you. It doesn't take a
mathematician to see that if you . . .

One, teach them to put on better talks,

Two, they'll sell their ideas better,and better ideas are what drive this business of ours.

A Complex Presentation

Target Audience

All those attending regional meetings.

Communication Objective

To create awareness within the target audience of the many avenues to improved margins.

Message

The squeeze play's on and we'll beat it by recognizing that good ideas are portable.

Tonality

Helpful, professional, optimistic.

Thank you and good morning, ladies and gentlemen.
Though most of you know me by now--at least
on sight--this is still my first regionwide formal talk to this organization.
And let me tell you, it's not as easy as it
looks.

SLIDE

In fact, putting it together reminds me of
what Yogi Berra once observed about baseball.
He said, "It's ninety percent hard work . . .
and the other half ain't easy."

SLIDE

Well, easy or not, it's a pleasure to be with
a group I know and respect.
I'm really glad to have found my way into
this wonderful business of ours.
Now you know, of course, with just a year in
the saddle, it's not possible to come on like an
industry guru, but by the same token, as Yogi
points out, "You can observe a lot just by
watching."
You don't need thirty years of experience in
this industry to know that there's a squeeze
play on.

SLIDE

And that if we're not careful, we could get
caught in the crunch between slipping volume and
rising costs.
As a business we have to make a choice and
the choice is this:
Are we going to meet the demands of the marketplace and still improve margins?
And the answer is, Yes!

SLIDE

Yes. We can build volume.
And yes, at the very same time . . .

SLIDE

We _can_ build margins.
I say yes not because I am hoping it's possible, but because, as the low-cost producers and
distributors, we have <u>already proved</u> and are
proving daily <u>it can be done</u>.
Today, profit success hinges on a delicate
balancing act between . . .

SLIDE

Infrastructure, controllable costs, and distribution.
Orchestrating <u>those</u> elements is what will deliver the profit improvement we desire--fifteen
percent per year.
So what I come to you with today are <u>ideas</u>,
ideas that have helped our fellow distributors.
But before we get to them, let's take a look
at our overall goals.

SLIDE

Our target is to achieve operating profit improvement of about fifteen percent in the current year.
Here's how we arrived at that number.
Our model calls for volume contribution to
increase five percent. The balance must come
from controllable cost improvement.
To meet our goals, gains need to be in the
neighborhood of seven to ten percent.

SLIDE

In the last several years, our operations
have developed the flagship performance cost
basis.

By operating on the basic premise that good ideas are portable, that what works in one region works in others, we can capture dozens and dozens of individual efficiency improvements made in this area or in that function.

Then extend those cost-saving ideas to others.

In a moment, I'm going to get into some of the ideas we are using to achieve flagship performance.

But before I do, I want to give you an idea of the magnitude of the savings that are on the table.

SLIDE

Last year total operating costs per case were two dollars and thirty-four cents. The theoretical flagship is one dollar and eighty-three cents.

Now, when you run the numbers out, the difference between the two . . .

The savings that result from achieving flagship costs amount to one hundred forty-seven million per year.

That's right! One hundred forty-seven million--more than fifty cents a case.

So much for goals.

The real question, the one hundred forty-seven million dollar question, is, how do we do it?

There are as many ways as there are operations.

Here's one approach.

Norman Bergdorf has developed a user-friendly software package that helps visualize the critical relationships between sales data and margins.

Let's take a look.

SLIDE

This slide shows what happened to margins when price was lowered to one seventy-nine on the top-selling package.

SLIDE

And this slide shows line managers the relationship between volume and margin from any cut
of the business--brands, packages, or accounts.
This is one good example out of hundreds--
maybe even thousands--of ways our group is better managing the business to improve margins.

SLIDE

Here's another.
Our plant in Paterson faced a classic case of
low volume and high cost and it looked as though
they would be forced to shut down their can op-
eration.
Meanwhile, the plant in south Jersey needed
upwards of two million cases a year to meet peak
demands.
The solution?
They sourced from Paterson.
Here's how it works.
Paterson installed a new Mead twelve twenty-
four wrap machine to multi-pak our requirements.
South Jersey supplies cans and ingredients.
Paterson receives a production fee.
Net, net, everybody wins.

SLIDE

And in the process, Paterson leveraged fixed
costs down via additional volume.

SLIDE

Here's another good example of how controllable cost management can be turned into a win-win
proposition.
Eastern Kentucky was faced with severe labor
problems and pressure on the environmental
front. They considered shutting down production.
Meanwhile, our Vernon operation was looking
to build their volume base to lower plant controlled cost.
The upshot was this.

SLIDE

Vernon began to source from Huntington on a
cost-effective basis. And the million plus cases
enabled Eastern to lower plant controlled cost
by sixteen percent.

SLIDE

Here's a case history of how good citizenship
makes good business.
The site is Rivington. The problem was landfill. Rivington, like most towns, is running out
of room.

SLIDE

Rivington manager Drake Albright figured that
by doing away with cardboard on the big package
and replacing it with reusable plastic shells,
he could eliminate three point seven million
pounds of corrugated and save three hundred and
sixty-five thousand cubic feet of landfill a
year.
So they converted . . .

SLIDE

And between materials and merchandising--they
saved double digits--twenty cents per case!

SLIDE REPRISE

Software . . .
Sourcing . . .
The only limit on saving controllable costs
is our imagination.
Remember, flagship performance isn't based on
one bold stroke. It's the combination of good
ideas that makes a real difference.
And when it comes to good ideas, don't forget
they're portable.
Look.

SLIDE

Another proven way to beat the distribution and selling cost squeeze is to maximize distribution productivity.

And here, with hand-held computers, we have found a means to save two to three cents per case simply by realizing efficiencies in the settlement process.

In addition, hand-held computers can help us capitalize on opportunities for further savings of as much as ten to fifteen cents per case.

SLIDE

Now, I'd like to turn to my final subject and that is the opportunity for infrastructure improvements.

This is our current pipeline. It involves all the steps from raw material supply to in-store activities.

Did you know that eighty to ninety-seven percent of labor activity adds little or no value in our operations?

That every package we produce is picked up and put down at least eleven times and as much as twenty-one times? Forty-one percent of the product that goes out comes back?

But here's the worst part: All the while these inefficiencies go on, from raw materials intake to in-store activities, the trade complains our service neither reflects consumer buying patterns nor meets their needs.

What's happening is that our infrastructure is not only costing us money--it's costing us customer good will.

SLIDE

Now look what happens when we focus on meeting customer needs and simplify the pipeline:

Minimum in-process materials, continuous, multistream blending, minimal finished goods warehousing, transport hauling, and satellite warehousing . . .

In other words, by streamlining the system, we not only meet customer needs better, we maximize sales and we create more in-store presence.

But that's not all we get.
There's a tangible savings to be gained, too.

SLIDE

A savings of between ten and twenty cents per case!
Ladies and gentlemen, beating the cost squeeze is and will remain our number one priority.
The goal is to get our costs down by some thirty to thirty-five cents over the next three years.
And the way it will happen is not through one bold stroke but through a combination of steps that involve

SLIDE

Controllable cost improvements, distribution cost improvements, and simplifying the structure.
It's a combination that means good things for everybody.
More money to reinvest in the business so we can beat the pants off a regionally threatening competitor.
More money to help us close the distribution gap and grow the business.
More money to spend against the consumer . . .
And yes, more money at the bottom line.
Yes, we're coming under fire, but that's nothing new.
We are good to begin with. Under fire we're even better. And as John Beach says in this month's company magazine, "If we're serious, we've got to work like we're all in the same boat."
Well, John, we are serious about this thing. We are all in the same boat and this is the launching point. Sharing and learning together-- in the end, that's how we're going to beat the squeeze play, and in the process, build the business.
Thank you.

A CEO's Recruiting Talk

Target Audience

All those attending meeting of the Marketing Club, Graduate School of Business, Harvard University.

Communication Objective

To create awareness within the target audience that the corporation regards human values as the most important of all.

Message

You represent the future of American business and the opportunity to talk with you is an opportunity to affect the future.

Tonality

Warm, engaging, thoughtful.

I'd like to thank all of you for your invitation. My mother always wanted me to go to Harvard, and you've made that possible. Of course, she wanted me to go for more than just a few hours!

Nevertheless, I am delighted to be here, and the real reason is because you ladies and gentlemen represent the future of American business. And the opportunity to talk with you is an opportunity to affect the future. I simply couldn't pass that up.

You've already heard a little bit about how well our corporation is doing, and perhaps you've had a chance to review some of the things that have been written about us lately. I don't think I'm giving away any company secrets when I tell you I see that success continuing.

I feel a little like one of the former head football coaches at the University of Miami, long before last Saturday's game. This particular fellow was big on innovation, and drilled into his players the need to innovate whenever they were faced with a critical situation.

Well, one time Miami had the ball on the opponent's five-yard line. They called an option play to the left. So Miami's quarterback--it was George Mira at that time--started rolling to his left. He suddenly spotted an open receiver, but there was just one little problem. Mira was right-handed, and a six-foot seven-inch two hundred seventy-five-pound tackle was hanging onto his right shoulder. But that didn't bother Mira.

Without a moment's hesitation, he switched the ball to his other hand, and threw the only left-handed pass of his life . . . for a touchdown.

The crowd went wild, and everyone along the sidelines was jumping up and down. Everyone but the coach; he just stood there very quietly. Finally, he turned to a newspaper reporter next to him and very matter-of-factly said, "Now, that's what I call coaching."

Well, we're not quite as calm and matter-of-fact about our success as that coach was about his. We're pretty pleased about how well we've done so far and excited about what the future still holds for us.

But the point is not that <u>we</u> are excited about our success, but that <u>you</u> should be excited about it. You should be excited because of <u>how</u> we've achieved success. It's not because of a few left-handed touchdown passes. It's because first, last, and always we're a <u>marketing</u> company. That's what we focus on. That's how we make our living.

You see, we don't sell commodities--bushels of corn or boxcars of wheat. We <u>market</u> big brands: names that pretty much define the market. We do it by using all the classic marketing tools: distribution, advertising, promotion. And they work.

And that's very important because, unlike penicillin or shoes or your daily bread, people can live without our products.

So why do people buy some thirty billion dollars worth each year? The answer is simple: <u>marketing</u>. That's what makes the difference for us.

So if any of you are wondering whether marketing is as hot a career today as it was yesterday, my answer is . . . you bet!

But I'm not here this afternoon to talk about marketing. You ladies and gentlemen know enough about that subject already. I'd rather talk about something that may be a little more personal and, at this stage of your life, perhaps even a little more interesting. I'd like to talk about what it takes to make a really successful career. With all the advantages you have-- intellect, drive, education--you'll have some success, no doubt. But will you reach your full potential and aspirations?

My point is this: What has worked so well for you so far inside <u>business school</u> may not necessarily achieve the same results for you, the same level of success, in <u>business</u>.

It occurred to me that when you make the transition from business school to business, you'll have to use a completely different set of muscles.

At our company, we spend a lot of time studying what makes people successful in our business. We don't do it out of any sense of academic curiosity, but for some very pragmatic business reasons. After all, we're successful only because our <u>people</u> are successful. And we <u>want</u> our people to be successful. We <u>need</u> them to be successful . . . to reach their <u>full</u> potential.

That means we're very concerned about the flip side of that: why some people fail in business, and why others, who are no better qualified in terms of education, commitment, and technical skills, succeed.

I'm not talking about the kind of failure where people are thrown out on the street. I'm talking about something more subtle; a kind of derailment; the failure to reach the full potential that your education and intelligence would suggest. I'm talking about people who have the capacity to be vice president of marketing at a fairly young age, but never rise above the director level. About the sensational young rookie who bats three ten, but who's capable of hitting three forty.

Perhaps a better way to look at it is this: Probably everybody who has ever graduated from Harvard Business School has the intelligence and the ambition to be the president or CEO of a major company or the leading "rainmaker" at an investment bank or agency. But not all of them reach that potential. Why not?

The six reasons we've identified may be a bit surprising. None of them has anything to do with technical skills, analytical ability or intellect. And none of them is automatically a fatal flaw. That's important.

If you look closely, you'll probably see evidence of some of these six factors in all of us. The way we avoid career derailment is knowing

ourselves and our shortcomings, and recognizing
the need to change or to manage around our
flaws. Success or failure still is in our own
hands.

The number one reason for failure is insen-
sitivity to other people! In other words, arrogance. It's the number one reason for failure in
business.

Arrogance is pretty bad anywhere, but it's
deadly in business. I'm talking about intelligent people who think no one else is intelligent. They think they have all the ideas and
that their way is the only way. Their mind
doesn't listen to any idea different from their
own. They don't learn how to improve their idea
when they have a good one. And they don't know
how to drop their idea when it's a bad one.

Of course, you can't just avoid being arro-
gant. That's not enough. You also have to learn
how to work with others. And there's an interesting psychological study that explains why.

It was done by two doctoral candidates at the
University of Washington. They assembled two
groups of people and told them they had survived
a plane crash in the desert. They had to find
some way to get back to safety.

One of the groups was given general guidelines about desert survival. The other was not.
But the untrained group did just as well as the
trained one. And the reason, according to the
psychological study, was that the untrained
group worked together as a team.

The same is true for surviving in business.
Teamwork is essential, and arrogance kills teamwork. Our success in marketing, in product development, our progress in everything we do is a
group enterprise.

That doesn't mean there isn't room for big
stars and soaring individual performances, or
that business is kind of a "go along to get
along" environment.

Far from it. The exact opposite is true. You
need big stars and exceptional performers. But
they must know how to tailor their performance
to fit a larger goal.

I could give plenty of examples of both kinds
of stars: the ones who create performance have
healthy egos and star quality written all over
them. But somehow they turn people on, not off.
They're superstars, all right. But, more important, they're superb team builders. And that's
why they reach the top.

The winners in a company, in a <u>successful</u>
company, are like the blades of a pair of
shears, joined together so they cannot be separated. Often moving in opposite directions, just
as often coming together. And when they do come
together, they're stronger than they ever were
apart. They cut through everything that comes
between them.

Just like a pair of shears, when people in a
company come together, when they work well together, the company becomes strongest. And
that's when you can cut through the competition.
And that's why teamwork is so important. In
fact, <u>essential</u> to business success. If you
can't build a team and get people to work together, you're never going to be the leader of
the band.

<u>Derailment number two</u>: playing politics, put-
ting your personal agenda above the common good.
That's death to a business.

Some people choose the side of an issue by
looking at who's on the other side. You know the
real trouble with these people? They're afraid.
They're so obsessed with advancing their own careers that they refuse to take chances. They
don't take a stand on an issue. They look for
the easy sell. And, like a weather vane, they
change their positions whenever the wind blows
in a different direction.

Of course, there's politics in any corporation, in any civic organization, in any church
group. That's just part of the dynamics of any

organization. The problem comes when people try
to manipulate others for their own gain and lose
sight of the organization's objectives.

We want people who do their homework. And who
decide on the basis of <u>what</u> they know, not <u>who</u>
they know. But even that's not enough. We also
want <u>commitment</u>. We have a saying that point-of-
view is worth ten I.Q. points. We need people
who aren't afraid to stand for something.

<u>Derailment number three</u>: inflexibility. I'm
talking about people who can't change their
ways. You know the people who are always shaking
their heads "no" in a meeting. Or worse, the
ones who give verbal agreement, but withhold any
real commitment. That's a sure way to fail.

There may be some jobs in this world that can
be filled by inflexible people, but they're not
in the consumer products industry.

Think about it: The consumer changes. The
competition changes. The market changes. Change
defines consumer marketing, and the man or woman
who can't handle change, who can't manage change
and anticipate change, is as dead as a Cabbage
Patch doll.

You've all heard the old adage: If it ain't
broke, don't fix it. That's terrible advice!
We're constantly fixing things that aren't broken, just to make them better.

And so earlier this year, we totally changed
our organization along regional lines. We created four autonomous businesses, each of which
is now responsible for <u>all</u> Pepsi operations--
franchised bottlers, company-owned operations,
and fountain syrup sales--within a geographic
area.

We think this new system makes us even more
responsive to the marketplace, and even more
competitive.

<u>Derailment number four</u>: can't take the heat.
We lose a surprising number of promising execu-

tives because they can't keep themselves under control when faced with pressure. They get hot when they should keep their cool. And they freeze when they should be on fire.

Their frustration is obvious. They get angry and that, in turn, alienates others. Their lack of control causes them to lose their focus on the issue. And it causes them and others to make bad decisions simply to get past the problem.

<u>Derailment number five</u>: lacking perseverance.

Some very good people have this problem. They have good ideas. They start well. They have a lot of things going for them. But they just run out of steam. They fail to get results.

Maybe they work so slowly that they allow the competition to catch up or to gain an advantage. Maybe they're reluctant to put in the extra time. Maybe they're more interested in the process than in the results.

Whatever else a successful executive has, he or she must have tenacity.

Persistence pays. Results come only when you are untiring, unrelenting, and unafraid to stay with something when you know you're right.

<u>Derailment number six</u>: lack of loyalty to the company.

I'm not talking about blind loyalty. People do have disagreements within a business about how it should be run or what strategic direction it should take. In fact, vigorous debate is essential to success. So I'm not talking about disagreement. I'm talking about disloyalty, about criticism behind the back, about people who constantly complain, but offer no suggestions for improvement. They may be unable to sell their own idea or unwilling to adapt to a new boss with a different style.

In a bigger sense, people who are disloyal can't be trusted at all because they lack integrity. I can't stress too much that in any business dealing integrity is the one glue that

holds everything together. I'm not just talking
about the obvious things, like stealing or cook-
ing the books. What I mean by integrity is an
openness, an honesty, a basic way of doing business.

So those are the six principal reasons why
people derail, why they gain less than their
full measure of success. Not because they're
dumb. Not because they have technical deficien-
cies. Not because they haven't mastered the
skills required for their job.

It's because of certain human qualities. It's
because of arrogance, playing politics, inflexi-
bility, inability to deal with pressure, lack of
perseverance, lack of loyalty.

These have nothing to do with intelligence or
experience or education or the college you attended. They have everything to do with character, with human interaction, with our ability to
deal with others, honestly and effectively.

And when you think about it, that's not surprising. You see, businesses--big business,
small business, corporations, agencies, investment banks--are all very human places.

Business is not theoretical, although theory
is important. But ideas by themselves won't get
the ball across the goal line. They won't set
the cash register ringing. Business is very emotional and very physical. It's buying and selling and showing up every day. It's dealing with
people's livelihoods. And that means dealing
with their lives. It requires sensitivity and
stamina and a lot of courage and character.

But success is never guaranteed, and issues
of character are sometimes easy to forget. I
don't want that to happen to any of you, especially if you come to work for us.

You see, there's a positive side to all of
this that's very, very exciting. Your diploma is
a ticket, a ticket to a lifelong journey through
the business world. It's a journey that should
be filled with personal growth, development, and
immense satisfaction.

But there's a trick to making the most of this journey. And our six causes for derailment should give you a hint of what it is.

If you focus too much on yourself and your career--the titles, the salary, the perks-- you're likely to run into a lot of issues that will cut your trip short.

But if you focus on the journey itself, on the people you work with, on the customers you serve, on getting better each and every day, on personal growth and development, your journey will be a long and rewarding one. And your career will take care of itself.

Thank you very much.

To Honor a Retiree

Target Audience

All those attending Partner's Dinner.

Communication Objective

To create awareness within the target audience that the retiree's presence will be missed.

Message

Part of him will always remain part of us.

Tonality

Proud and sad.

In a few days, Harry Johnson will walk out the doors of this institution we call a partnership.

When he does, he will not leave alone.

With him will march the accumulated memories of twenty-six years of sharing his own light to add luster to ours.

That much is inevitable.

But happily, not so important.

What does count is what remains--the presence that he stirs in us, inspires in us, to fight not just for what is correct but for what is right.

So you see, in the end, he does not really leave.

He cannot.

Part of the him who goes will always be part of the us who remain.